Six Irish Poets

Six Irish Poets

---❖---

AUSTIN CLARKE

RICHARD KELL

THOMAS KINSELLA

JOHN MONTAGUE

RICHARD MURPHY

RICHARD WEBER

---❖---

EDITED BY ROBIN SKELTON

LONDON
OXFORD UNIVERSITY PRESS
NEW YORK   TORONTO
1962

Oxford University Press, Amen House, London E.C. 4

GLASGOW NEW YORK TORONTO MELBOURNE WELLINGTON
BOMBAY CALCUTTA MADRAS KARACHI LAHORE DACCA
CAPE TOWN SALISBURY NAIROBI IBADAN ACCRA
KUALA LUMPUR HONG KONG

75/68

CONTENTS

v

THOMAS KINSELLA

JOHN MONTAGUE

vi

ACKNOWLEDGEMENTS

AUSTIN CLARKE. All the poems included in this volume appear in *Later Poems* (Dolmen Press, 1961); some have been printed in the *Irish Times*.

RICHARD KELL. All these poems, except 'Landfall', have been published before. 'Kierkegaard', 'The Balance', 'Poet on the Brink', 'Fishing Harbour Towards Evening', 'The Swan', 'The Quarrel and the Jester', 'A Word for my Son', 'Time for Clipping', and 'Going Anywhere?' all appear in *Control Tower* (Chatto & Windus, 1962); 'Kierkegaard' has also appeared in *Outposts*; 'Note for an Imaginary Diary' and 'Spring Night' in *Rann*; 'In the Beginning' in *Irish Writing*; 'The Quarrel and the Jester' and 'Going Anywhere?' in the *Listener*; 'A Word for my Son' on the *Third Programme*; 'Time for Clipping' in the *New Statesman*; 'Memorandum for Minos' and 'The Swan' in *Fantasy Press Poets No. 35* (1956); 'Gospels' in the *Observer*, and 'The Makers' in *Poetry and Audience*.

THOMAS KINSELLA. The poems included here have been published as follows: 'Another September' has appeared in *Irish Writing*, *Borestone Mountain Poetry Awards 1958*, *Another September* (Dolmen Press, 1958), and *Poems and Translations* (Atheneum Press, U.S.A., 1961); 'In the Ringwood' in *Icarus*, *Another September*, and *Poems and Translations*; 'Two Moralities' in the *Irish Times*, *Poems and Translations*, and *Moralities* (Dolmen Press, 1960); 'Baggot Street Deserta' in *Poetry Now* (Faber), *Irish Writing*, *Another September*, and *Poems and Translations*; 'Thinking of Mr. D.' in the *Sunday Independent*, *Guinness Book of Poetry 1958*, *An Anthology of Modern Verse 1940–1960* (Methuen, 1961), *Another September*, and *Poems and Translations*; 'A Portrait of the Engineer' in *Poems and Translations*; 'Wedding Morning' in the *Kilkenny Magazine* and *Poems and Translations*; 'Mirror in February' in *Poetry* (Chicago); 'A Country Walk' in *The Dolmen Miscellany of Irish Writing* (Dolmen Press, 1962).

JOHN MONTAGUE Ten of these poems appeared in *Poisoned Lands* (MacGibbon & Kee, 1961); of these, 'A Footnote on Monasticism' was also in *Forms of Exile* (Dolmen Press, 1958); 'Wild Sports of the West' in the *Irish Times* and the *Listener*; 'Like Dolmens Round My Childhood, the Old People' and 'The Water Carrier' in *Threshold*; 'A Royal Visit' in the *Kilkenny Magazine*; 'Old Mythologies' in *Poetry* and the *Times Literary Supplement*; 'Poisoned Lands' and 'The First Invasion of Ireland' in *Carleton Miscellany*; 'Woodtown Manor' in *Studies*. Of the three new poems, 'Reconstruction' and 'The Country Fiddler' appeared in *Encounter*, and 'Paris: April, 1961' in the *Irish Times*.

RICHARD MURPHY. These poems are all to be included in *Sailing to an Island* (Faber, 1963); the Dolmen Press published separately 'Sailing to an Island' (1955 and 1961), 'The Last Galway Hooker' (1961), and 'The Woman of the House' (1959); 'Girl at the Seaside' and 'The Philosopher and the Birds' were in *The Archaeology of Love* (Dolmen Press, 1955); 'The Cleggan Disaster' is included in *The Dolmen Miscellany of Irish Writing* (Dolmen Press, 1962). 'Years Later' (from 'The Cleggan Disaster') has won first prize in the Guinness Awards 1962. Magazines and anthologies where these poems previously appeared include *Adelphi*, *The Bell*, *Encounter*, *English Love Poems* (Faber), the *Irish Times*, *Listen*, the *Listener*, *Poetry at the Mermaid*, *Poetry* (Chicago), *Poetry Now* (Faber), and the *Yale Review*.

RICHARD WEBER. 'Lady and Gentleman' appeared in the *Irish Times* and the *Dubliner*; 'Portrait of a Statesman' in part in the *Times Literary Supplement*, and in entirety in the *Dubliner*; 'Hampstead Heath' is included in the *Dolmen Miscellany of Irish Writing* (Dolmen Press, 1962); 'Shaw House' and 'The Lion and O'Reilly' were in *Threshold*; 'O'Reilly's Reply', 'In Memoriam', and 'Summa Theologica' all appeared in *Delta*, and part of 'In Memoriam' was also in *Irish Writing*; 'The Flight of the Wild Geese' and 'A Life' have been in the *Dubliner*; 'The Wave' has been in the *Irish Times*, 'On an Italian Hillside' in the *Kilkenny Magazine*, and 'The Travellers' in *Satis*.

INTRODUCTION

THIS anthology does not claim to be representative of all the kinds of poetry being written by Irishmen at present; its object is simply to give enough space to six good poets to enable them to introduce themselves to new readers more completely than is possible in the cramped confines of the usual sort of compilation. It is difficult for any poetry reader, however dedicated, to get to know the work of all the poets who have aroused his interest by single poems in periodicals. Young poets, in particular, are hard to get to know for their publications are often hard to find, and are sometimes discreetly ephemeral. This, then, is an attempt to group together a selection of poems by six Irish poets, some of whom are still little known, and by so doing give an opportunity to new readers to make up their minds about them on the basis of a reasonable amount of evidence.

The choice of poets is, I must emphasize, purely personal. There are several good poets who could have been included, but are not. Guilty as I feel about these omissions, I would have felt more guilty had I failed to give adequate space to each poet here. I can only apologize for the limitations upon space which made exclusions necessary, and express special regret that it proved impossible to include any work by Patrick Kavanagh; I do not apologize for any of my inclusions.

Looking through the collection, I notice that, while all the poets are Irish, there are vast differences of approach; though each poet here has devoted some space to what might be described as purely national themes, each poet has handled those themes differently. Mr. Austin Clarke, the oldest poet in the collection, and a man whose eminence has been long recognized, was born in 1896 in Dublin. Alone of the poets here, he has experienced both British and Irish rule in his country. As a young man he watched the battle of the Post Office during the Easter Rising of 1916. He has lived in an Ireland intensely conscious of its nationalism, and also experienced the more international outlook of the time before the Rebellion, and that of today. It may be this that has turned him, in so many of his later poems, towards the consideration of exactly what values are to be found in the country in which he lives. He has seen the country created, and, therefore, is less inclined to accept it blindly, and more inclined to question, satirize, and judge.

It has been very difficult to make a selection of Mr. Clarke's later poems, for they should properly be read in bulk, each poem contributing towards a panoramic whole of extraordinary range and passion. A small selection such as this cannot hope to do justice to his work; I can only hope that it does not fall so far short as to appear a falsification.

The impulse towards observation of society, and towards the analysis of whatever is most 'Irish', can also be seen in the work of John Montague. Mr. Montague was born in 1929 in Brooklyn, New York, of Irish parents, but he came to Ireland at the age of four to spend his childhood on an Ulster farm. He spent most of his later life in Dublin, but has recently moved to Paris with his French wife. Here is, perhaps, an example of the international outlook, which I have mentioned, yet Mr. Montague finds himself frequently harking back to the Ulster of his childhood, trying to identify what it has meant to him, and trying to explore and explain the values of the Irish countryside as he knew it. In these poems he is representative of much Irish poetry of our century; the same impulse has been shared by Patrick Kavanagh, F. R. Higgins, John Hewitt, and many more.

Richard Murphy also concerns himself largely with Irish themes, but he seems less to judge than to celebrate. In his long poems, 'The Last Galway Hooker' and 'The Woman of the House', he is creating memorials rather than asking for verdicts. He was born in the west of Ireland in 1927, but lived in Ceylon for the greater part of the first seven years of his life. He was educated in England, and has spent some time in the Bahamas and in Crete. For a number of years now, however, he has lived on the west coast of Ireland, where he owns the hooker of his poem, in which he earns his living by taking visitors out sea-fishing during the tourist season. His work is highly individual, and full of strong lucid imagery which makes the scenes and people he describes completely convincing.

Thomas Kinsella has also attacked the problem of summing up something about his own country, particularly in his long poem 'A Country Walk'. He is, however, at a first glance less obviously concerned with Irishry than many of his fellows, although he is himself one of the best modern translators of Ancient Irish literature. He was born in Dublin in 1928, where he still lives, and where he works as a civil servant. His work has immense discipline and strength, and in his meditation 'Baggot Street Deserta' he shows an easy control and dexterity which are masterly. His work is, perhaps, as much in the English as in the Irish tradition. He does not often make use of the techniques of internal rhyme and alliteration which are to be found in Gaelic verse, and in this is unlike both Austin Clarke and Richard Weber.

Richard Weber was born in 1932 in Dublin, where he now works, after spending some time in London and Italy. He differs from many poets in deliberately using several different manners, and in allowing his poetry to range widely from private to public matters. His interest in alliterative techniques can be seen in the extraordinarily rich and disciplined structure of 'Lady and Gentleman'. He does, however, add to his interest in Gaelic techniques an interest in Ireland as a whole. His character O'Reilly speaks for himself in this respect. Mr. Weber has not yet produced a book of his own, though he has produced two pamphlets and a broadsheet, so this is his first appearance between hard covers with more than one or two poems.

Richard Kell's first book has only recently appeared. He was born in Youghal, Co. Cork, in 1927, but lived in India from the time he was two years old until he was seven. The following nineteen years were spent entirely in Ireland, but his recent years have been spent in London. Mr. Kell's work is much more domestic in its attitudes than the work of some of his fellows. His poems appear to arise out of the commonplaces of the day, which he sees with penetration, and which he describes and explores with force and wit. He too, however, cannot avoid writing many poems specifically about Ireland.

I have harped upon the way in which all these poets use, to a greater or lesser extent, specifically Irish themes, because it seems to me that this is both healthy and interesting. It is healthy, for it shows that Irish poetry can still base itself firmly upon what might be described as 'natural resources'. It is interesting because in England at present there appear to be very few poets indeed with this kind of awareness of their nationality, this sense of belonging, however rebelliously, to a social or ethnic group. Such an awareness can, of course, lead to regionalism of the bad, or parochial kind; it can, however, also lead to real vitality, as I believe it has in the poetry in this book. The sense of belonging is, I believe, important to poetry. It gives it a firm foundation upon which to build. It gives it roots. And, however far the poets here represented have ranged, either in their words or in their lives, it is clear that they find in national concerns, and in Irish scenes, something which perpetually fascinates and disturbs.

ROBIN SKELTON

AUSTIN CLARKE

NO RECOMPENSE

QUALITY, number and the sweet divisions
Of reason may forget their schoolmen now,
And door-chill, body's heat, anger of vein,
Bring madness in our sleep. I have endured
The enmity of my own mind that feared
No argument; but O when truth itself
Can hold a despairing tongue, what recompense
To find my name in any mortal mouth?

OFFERINGS

PITY poor souls long suffering
In Purgatory, try to name
The living ones in crowded street.
What light can any stranger borrow
From them? Soon, very soon, we fade
As memory when our small savings
Are gone and every Mass is said.
And now in city churches, few
Pay little visits for our sake
At dusk. The candle-box is filled
With other pennies. In the morning,
Black alb is worn for eyelids that carry
In quiet tears the newly dead.

PILGRIMAGE

No bed that walks is worth such pain:
The aeroplane that sinks from earth,
Arteries faster than railway train,
Ship-loads dipping with baggage, berth;
Sickness below and in the clouds:
Too many thousands are brought to pray
Because our wonder must have crowds
Purchasing trifles at stall and tray
To make a holiday of hope,
Then, stare at stretcher, limbs that grope.

CHRISTMAS EVE

Dublin: 1959

Crack-up . . . crack-down. Guttering squib
Unhallowed the street-light of the Crib,
Our shops had bought for Mary and Son
In hope of larger benison.
Though every firework has been banned,
Student or reeler from a band
Flung it. Could fizzle-fazzle refuse
Merry, unlawful touch of fuse?
Go-bang alarmed, in the traffic, an
Elderly crosser, girl, African
Converted by us. Bar-clamouring booze
Came, mobbing O'Connell Street with boos,
Mocking the ancient jars of Cana,
So how could the Garda Siochana
Defend authority in pairs
From youths with thrown-out apples, pears,
Our goodness rotting in their teens?
Quick reinforcements from canteens,
They say, scoring with stripes and licks,
Batoned their fellow-Catholics,
Perhaps a running Protestant
Or two (not many are extant),
Piously making no arrest,
For bloody rioters need a rest
In hospital. Swayed by the mass,
Standers were late for Midnight Mass.

EARLY UNFINISHED SKETCH

ROSALIND, in a négligé,
Began to sketch me as I lay
Naked and soon her serious touch
On sheet delighted me as much
In art as loving. Pencil drew,
Poised, measured again, sped downward, flew
Like love scattering clothes to greet
Itself. The outline was complete.
She pondered. Detail was different,
More difficult. She seemed intent
On what the ancients had adored,
Christian apologists deplored.
'Finish it, pet, how can I wait?'
'But, darling, I must concentrate.'
She failed, fled back to our caresses,
Sat up.
     'What's wrong?'
            'The problem presses.
I have it! Yes. That group in bronze.'
'The satyrs?'
     'Herrick would call them fauns.
Stock-still—'
     'in the fountain spray at Florence.'
'All tourists showing their abhorrence!'
'But if that sculptor dared to limn it—'
'The nude, today, must have a limit.'
'And Rosalind—'
     'obey the laws
Of decency.'
     'In the line she draws?'

THE DEAD SEA SCROLLS

WHY should our scholars try to save
The lost, because an Arab boy
Found too much goodness in a cave?
No looking back will change our Lot,
Make Paul a pry. Can bits destroy
Our great succession with blot and jot?
We know the gloss on a brown skin.
Many suspect that fire and sin
Have something in a bigger pot.

WAR PROPAGANDA

NEIGHBOURING metal may summon the drum,
But ear, beware. They preach too well
Who choose the text of Kingdom come.
Rope-swung victims ring that bell.

RESPECTABLE PEOPLE

THOUGHT rattles along the empty railings
Of street and square they lived in, years
Ago. I dream of them at night,
Strangers to this artificial light,
Respectable people who gave me sweets,
Talked above my head or unfobbed
The time. I know them by each faded
Smile and their old-fashioned clothes.
But how can I make room for them
In a mind too horrible with life?
This is the last straw in the grave,
Propping the tear in which grief burns
Away. Shame of eternity
Has stripped them of their quiet habits,
Unshovelled them out of the past.
Memory finds beyond that last
Improvidence, their mad remains.

THE STRAYING STUDENT

On a holy day when sails were blowing southward,
A bishop sang the Mass at Inishmore,
Men took one side, their wives were on the other
But I heard the woman coming from the shore:
And wild in despair my parents cried aloud
For they saw the vision draw me to the doorway.

Long had she lived in Rome when Popes were bad,
The wealth of every age she makes her own,
Yet smiled on me in eager admiration,
And for a summer taught me all I know,
Banishing shame with her great laugh that rang
As if a pillar caught it back alone.

I learned the prouder counsel of her throat,
My mind was growing bold as light in Greece;
And when in sleep her stirring limbs were shown,
I blessed the noonday rock that knew no tree:
And for an hour the mountain was her throne,
Although her eyes were bright with mockery.

They say I was sent back from Salamanca
And failed in logic, but I wrote her praise
Nine times upon a college wall in France.
She laid her hand at darkfall on my page
That I might read the heavens in a glance
And I knew every star the Moors have named.

Awake or in my sleep, I have no peace now,
Before the ball is struck, my breath has gone,
And yet I tremble lest she may deceive me
And leave me in this land, where every woman's son
Must carry his own coffin and believe,
In dread, all that the clergy teach the young.

AN EARLY START

WIDE-AWAKE, suddenly, as that new clang there,
I clapped my ears beneath the bedclothes, guessing
The Fathers of the Holy Ghost had bought
A bigger bell. Why should our blessed truth
Be measured by the mile? When I was humble,
My lies were quietly sung and never paid,
Yet they have made my bed. I will lie on,
Refuse to count a stroke. Troubler, your tongue
Is silver, though it rust. Strike if you must
And rattle every penny in the house.

INSCRIPTION FOR A HEADSTONE

WHAT Larkin bawled to hungry crowds
Is murmured now in dining-hall
And study. Faith bestirs itself
Lest infidels in their impatience
Leave it behind. Who could have guessed
Batons were blessings in disguise,
When every ambulance was filled
With half-killed men and Sunday trampled
Upon unrest? Such fear can harden
Or soften heart, knowing too clearly
His name endures on our holiest page,
Scrawled in a rage by Dublin's poor.

VANISHING IRISH

POVERTY drew lip down and yet there was laughter
In that raggedness of ours. Blind Raftery,
Who knew man's charges are both long and short,
Clapped heat to the touch-hole of the mighty mortar
Once—sent a young fellow, with shirt-tails flying the flag
Of his country, in search of bare toes and a shawl as bedraggled.
But how could he marry? His only belongings were longings,
Hugs, squeezes, kisses, a hundred thousand strong.
And how can I tell of his journey? Our silence now
Is beyond the aim of words and telltale frowned on.
Somewhere, the last of our love-songs found a refuge.
Perhaps in the hall of Rhadamanthus, the deaf
Can hear the comeback of its fol-de-rol
Skipping around the monstrous, unseen columns,
Free from our burden of bad thoughts and gloating,
Content as a flea in Connemara petticoat.

THE ENVY OF POOR LOVERS

PITY poor lovers who may not do what they please
With their kisses under a hedge, before a raindrop
Unhouses it; and astir from wretched centuries,
Bramble and briar remind them of the saints.

Her envy is the curtain seen at night-time,
Happy position that could change her name.
His envy—clasp of the married whose thoughts can be alike,
Whose nature flows without the blame or shame.

Lying in the grass as if it were a sin
To move, they hold each other's breath, tremble,
Ready to share that ancient dread—kisses begin
Again—of Ireland keeping company with them.

Think, children, of institutions mured above
Your ignorance, where every look is veiled,
State-paid to snatch away the folly of poor lovers
For whom, it seems, the sacraments have failed.

USUFRUCT

THIS house cannot be handed down.
Before the scriven ink is brown,
Clergy will sell the lease of it.
I live here, thinking, ready to flit
From Templeogue, but not at ease.
I hear the flood unclay the trees,
Road-stream of traffic. So does the midge,
With myriads below the bridge,
Having his own enormous day,
Unswallowed. Ireland was never lay.
My mother wore no rural curch
Yet left her savings to the Church,
That she might aid me by-and-by,
Somewhere beyond the threatening sky.
What could she do, if such in faith
Be second nature? A blue wraith
That exquisites the pool, I mean
The kingfisher, too seldom seen,
Is warier than I am. Flash
Of inspiration makes thought rash.

THE TRIAL OF ROBERT EMMET

to be re-enacted
at Green Street Courthouse
for An Tóstal, 1956

SENTENCE the lot and hurry them away,
The court must now be cleared, batten and spot
Swung up with rope and ladder, lighting-plot
Rehearsed. No need of drop-scene for the play
To-night: bench, box and bar in well-mixed ray
Make do. Though countless miscreants have got
A life-term here, and some, the scaffold knot,
Forget the cells our safety fills by day.
See British greed and tyranny defied
Once more by that freethinker in the dock
And sigh because his epitaph remains
Unwritten. Cheer revolution by the clock
And lastly—badge and holy metal guide
Your cars home, hooting through our dirtiest lanes.

MORTAL PRIDE

When thought of all our thought has crossed
The mind in pain, God only knows
What we must suffer to be lost,
What soul is called our own.
Before the truth was hid in torment,
With nothing but this mortal pride,
I dreamed of every joy on earth
And shamed the angel at my side.

Pray, how shall any bride discover
A husband in the state of bliss,
Learn in the curious arms of love
The ancient catechism
Man must obey? She never fears
He will forget the sacrament.
But thought is older than the years:
Before our doom, it came and went.

SUMMER LIGHTNING

THE heavens opened. With a scream
The blackman at his night-prayers
Had disappeared in blasphemy,
And iron beds were bared;
Day was unshuttered again,
The elements had lied,
Ashing the faces of mad men
Until God's likeness died.

Napoleon took his glittering vault
To be a looking-glass.
Lord Mitchell, pale and suffering,
Fell to the floor in halves.
The cells were filling. Christopher
O'Brien, strapped in pain,
For all the rage of syphilis,
Had millions in his brain.

James Dunn leaped down the dormitory,
Thought has no stopping-place,
His bright bed was a corner shop,
Opening, closing, late.
Behind a grille, the unfrocked priest
Had told his own confession:
Accidents in every street
Rang the Angelus.

Flight beyond flight, new stories flashed
Or darkened with affliction
Until the sweet choir of Mount Argus
Was heard at every window,

Was seen in every wing. The blackman
Kept laughing at his night-prayers
For somebody in white had taken
His photograph downstairs.

When sleep has shot the bolt and bar,
And reason fails at midnight,
Dreading that every thought at last
Must stand in our own light
Forever, sinning without end:
I pity, in their pride
And agony of wrong, the men
In whom God's likeness died.

PENAL LAW

Burn Ovid with the rest. Lovers will find
A hedge-school for themselves and learn by heart
All that the clergy banish from the mind,
When hands are joined and head bows in the dark.

THE LUCKY COIN

COLLECT the silver on a Sunday,
Weigh the pennies of the poor,
His soul can make a man afraid
And yet thought will endure.
But who can find by any chance
A coin of different shape
That never came from Salamanca
Or danced on chapel plate?

Though time is slipping through all fingers
And body dare not stay,
That lucky coin, I heard men tell it,
Had glittered once in Galway
And crowds were elbowing the spirit
While every counter shone,
Forgetting grief until the ages
Had changed it for a song.

Turning in cartwheels on the fairground,
The sun was hastier—
That strolling girls might have for dowry,
Two hands about a waist;
Men voted for the Liberator
After the booths were closed
And only those in failing health
Remembered their own souls.

On Nephin many a knot was tied,
The sweet in tongue made free there,
Lovers forgot on the mountain-side
The stern law of the clergy

That kiss, pinch, squeeze, hug, smack denied,
Forgot the evil, harm
And scandal that comes closer, lying
In one another's arms.

Not one of us will ever find
That coin of different shape
For it was lost before our rising
Or stolen—as some say.
But when our dread of the unseen
Has rifled hole and corner,
How shall we praise the men that freed us
From everything but thought.

RICHARD KELL

KIERKEGAARD

'Without the risk, faith is an impossibility'

I HAVE three plans to choose from on this island,
And every one a risk. Should I sail forth
With scant provisions in a tiny boat,
And set my course toward the crystal north,
Drowned or starved the loss I bear is double.
And so it is if I should seek the south,
Plodding through jungle, swamp and treacherous desert,
No wand of water touch my withered mouth,
And vultures pick the autumn from my bones.
If neither sea nor sand should make my grave,
But lazy I watch this palm-tree dust the moon,
I tempt the fury of the tidal wave.

But no, he says: though three alternatives,
You have a single choice: to put to sea
And aim your bows toward the grim horizon,
While love is softly washing on the lee.
There is no time to rummage in reflection
Or lust and lounge with animal aplomb.
(The big green book lies open on my hand
And ticks away the seconds like a bomb).

THE BALANCE

ALWAYS the one that will not let me be—
When I would overflow (the mind free,
The heart ready to love, the voice to sing),
Reminds me with its prudent nagging tongue

That life is such and such: the free mind,
The loving heart and singing voice are kind;
So plan, cherish, be provident, pay the bills:

The horses lumber, but the tiger kills.

Always the one that will not let me change—
When I'd be careful, sympathize, arrange
(The voice level, the mind about to freeze),
Recalls what goodness tamed no longer sees,

That life is such and such: the frozen mind,
The level voice are to themselves unkind;
Then play, be prodigal, give joy its head:

The fountain's reckless, but the cistern's dead.

POET ON THE BRINK

CALM autumn night, seen from a high window:
Above the roofs, the trees, an urban sky
Breathed-on and fogged with light; a notched horizon
Printed black; spread behind leaves, transparent
Fans of lamp-gold; a clock-tower, white as bone,
Rapt in a floodlit trance; and over all
A gritty hush, a solvent monotone.

The clock strikes peace—and any moment now
West 3 will beg a sonnet. Just remember
What's going on down there, and let it beg.
Most certainly the very houses seem,
And all that mighty heart is lying—still.
Even amid such trees the fluting owl
Glides velvet through the darkness to his kill.

FISHING HARBOUR TOWARDS EVENING

Slashed clouds leak gold. Along the slurping wharf
The snugged boats creak and seesaw. Round the masts

Abrasive squalls flake seagulls off the sky:
Choppy with wings the rapids of shrill sound.

Wrapt in spliced airs of fish and tar,
Light wincing on their knives, the clockwork men

Incise and scoop the oily pouches, flip
The soft guts overboard with blood-wet fingers.

Among three rhythms the slapping silver turns
To polished icy marble upon the deck.

THE SWAN

NOTHING more serene than the fluid neck,
The body curved like snow on foliage,
And spilt reflection moving smooth as oil.

But something wrecks the tranquil certainty:
The clean-cut shape unfolds; an evil wind
Tears its roots out of the fertile water.

The pattern's tugged awry—the neck rammed stiff,
Cumbrous wings whacking the startled air—
And terror swirls the surface of the lake.

NOTE FOR AN IMAGINARY DIARY

ONCE, to laze the weeks away like this,
Stealing a moment more of truancy,
Another after that on the slightest pretext,
Seemed allowed or even willed by God—
Yet needed no doctrine of predestination.

Somehow, it seemed, nothing could go far wrong.
Well, if it wasn't God's idea, at least
A job not done, a fear not overcome,
An easy pleasure seized at the last moment
Simply couldn't matter much in the end.

For this was Me. Whom some vague destiny
Had favoured with a special kind of schedule:
So if I chuffed a while on sleepy looplines
Or even jumped the track for half a day,
I'd still arrive at the proper place and time.

Playing hookey's dangerous now. But still
The sensual fool persists in quaint notions,
Such as: knowing at last the risk you run,
Will you have the guts to go on choosing
The loafer's way, the least exacting pleasure?

(How well the tempter knows the lyric poet,
Who's never sure the fool is not the sage).
When I would answer, two things bother me:
The highwire stretching from belief to action;
The fact, if such it is, that I am free.

IN THE BEGINNING

GOD was the first poem ever uttered
By innocent astonished lips when doubt
Had dropped a pebble in the water's trance,
The image of Narcissus cracked and rippled.
Then nothing was itself. Always the hunters
Prowled through metaphor, felt it underfoot
Or brushing across their shoulders; saw it burst
Above the jungle, slash the trees with rain,
Dispensing love and anger like a giant.

And every poem was a souvenir
Of the unending trek toward perfection
(Lying surely beyond the steaming ridges,
The poisoned tracts of swamp). The eyes that once
Like emeralds caught the light of simple beauty
Were shaded now with terror, and the young
Smooth stems of thought crumpled and cut like thorn-trees;
And all day long among the voiceless flowers,
The sunlight's tilted pillars, parrots gossiped,
And screeched with laughter at the goggling idols.

(For Muriel)

SPRING NIGHT

OUT on Killiney Hill that night, you said
'Remember how we promised to come up here
When snow is lying under a full moon?'
And I made no reply—to hide my sadness,
Thinking we might not satisfy that whim,
Ever perhaps, at least for years to come,
Since it was spring, and winter would see us parted.

Sitting on the Druid's Chair recalled
The last time we were there, a night of icy
Wind and moonlight when the sea was churning
Silver and the distant hills were clear;
How we belonged to them and they to us.
Now there was no brightness—only a vast
Obscurity confusing sea and sky,
Dalkey Island and the lights of Bray
Submerged and suffocating in the mist.

And there was no belonging now; no vivid
Elemental statement to compel
Refusal or assent, making decision
Easy; but a dumb neutrality
That challenged us to give it character
And view our own minds large as a landscape.
To you it was tranquil. Sinister to me.

Lying under the pine tree, looking up
At the small stars and breathing the wood's sweetness,
We spoke hardly a word. I could not tell you
I was afraid of something out there

In the future, like that dark and bitter sea;
And how my love for you would have me lonely
Until the fear was broken. I could say
'Be close to me this winter and every winter;
We'll come up here to watch the snow by moonlight'—
And that would be too easy. For I must give
To you whose meaning transcends moods and moments
Nothing half-hearted or ambiguous,
But the perfected diamond of my will.

THE QUARREL AND THE JESTER

HARDLY as tall
Even as the kitchen table.
A pint-size chucklehead
With a language of three words,
A blithe, believing eye,
A six-inch stride.

Something is going on
That's over his head. He trots
From knee to knee, drawing
Out of the unsuspected
Cold of the upper world
Familiar warmth.

And like the fool
(Without the fool's cunning)
Keeps out of politics:
When rival courtiers glare
Turns the indifferent glass
To any face,

Recalling there
The quaint humanity.
In his bright underworld
Something is going on:
He brings from fool to fool
Their common love.

A WORD FOR MY SON

I

LOOK, the first reel
Run off in memory, all
The bad bits cut away:
Discoveries, thrills!—the feel
Of ice cream on your tongue,
The hop of a red ball.

Half-hours of trains that sprout
From sleepy distances,
Bore through the wind, expand,
Smash your taut trance, a clout
Of steam-and-metal thunder
That crumbles, sifts, dies.

Barges down the canal,
Dock-leaves on glossy folds
Of water launched and lilted,
The sunned air magical;
By dandelion clocks
The timeless hours told.

You at the airport, spellbound.
Tension of noise and speed,
Slipstream playing the ground
Glissando: floated clear
On the smooth modulation
The sun-slicked wings recede.

Richmond, Windsor, Kew:
Long days of crowds and steamers,
Picnics and daffodils.
Your eyes alive with new
Puzzlements and convictions,
Your sleeping rich with dreams.

II

The deadlife now: the flint.
Rare things are filed away
Marked 'useless, treat with care',
The seemly trash we stint
And hate for reinstated.
A man has bills to pay.

A child has things to learn
Other than joy. (Not I,
Not any human being,
Authorized this). The turn
Of time leaves stinking pools
Where poisons multiply.

You four, I thirty-two:
I know but do not feel
The way you feel. That knowledge
Is my best gift to you
When love is mean, and pity
A construct of the will.

Yours is the same person
That prowled my ruined hours,
Fretting in shadows, dodging
The white floodbeam of reason.
By the same twist you change
And brood, contentment sours.

Watching you sulk and whine,
Your sense of wonder blurred,
Where shall I seek—knowing
The demon also mine
And you too young for knowledge—
The purifying word?

TIME FOR CLIPPING

On our arrival they were merely green
Needles pricking the soil, with space between
For air and sunlight; pride of the previous owner
Who, dreaming a lawn quite innocent of weeds,
Had cleared the ground, sprinkled the fine seeds
And left the rest to fate and gardener's honour.

For thirty weeks they grew undisciplined,
Guzzling the rain and grappling with the wind;
Each juicy filament took the lean and swerve
Of its compacting wave in a churned lake.
At last, fetching the clippers and the rake,
I contemplate the sentence I must serve.

And then the blades move in, precise and swift,
Chopping the tough lank fibres, and a drift
Of shredded silk is loosed above the whish
And clack of the clean steel. In tangles wet
With hoarded rain—refusing to forget—
Their fragrance lingers like a mindless wish.

At length we make our survey: sodden dirt,
A stubble grimed, uneven, but alert;
And there the slugs and earthworms that remain
Through all retrenchments. Yet no real weed
Is trundled out of consciousness to feed
The slow impartial bonfire down the lane.

GOING ANYWHERE?

THE limousine that Mr. L. S. Dee,
Tortured with ulcers and insomnia,
Works like a slave to earn enough to run
Is indispensably related to
His job of marketing accessories
For the equipment used in setting up
The plant essential to producers of
An automatic measuring device
Particularly favoured by those firms
That specialize in intricate machines
For companies that make a certain type
Of electronic instrument designed
To regulate a mechanism required
By factories that supply materials
Used in the shaping of precision tools
Connected with the processes involved
In manufacturing refrigerators:
Cold comfort for such perishable foods
As now enrich the breakfast Mr. Grim
Savours without conviction, being sick
From an anxiety neurosis due
To his employment in the firm that made
The limousine that Mr. L. S. Dee,
Tortured with ulcers and insomnia,
Works like a slave to earn enough to run . . .

MEMORANDUM FOR MINOS

INFLATED boys, when clergymen are odd,
Compress with handkerchiefs their bulging laughter.

(As children in the bathroom torture taps,
Stubbing explosive water with their thumbs.)

So congregations chained in sulphurous pews
Might gag their giggling through an endless sermon.

GOSPELS

Under its hump, the town
Straggles beside dun sand
Where the ebb tide uncovers
Seaweed and slimy stone.
Fairylights, fountain, bandstand
Play the uneasy lovers.

The ingrown hungers rage.
Hot sermons, anodyne
Of hymns, disturb the patter
Of the hypnotist on the stage.
Tranced lips guzzle wine
From glasses filled with water.

Pure streams from granite ledges
Fall to the town and swill
Flat shingle solitudes
Beyond the last bridges.
Impenetrably still
The black mountain broods.

THE MAKERS

THE artisan didn't collect his gear and say
'What beautiful object shall I make today?'

The poet didn't fondle a phrase and gape,
And think 'What elegant structure can I shape?'

The artisan made a gatepost
So that a certain gate could be opened and closed.

The poet started a poem
So that a meaning could reveal a form.

The gatepost is itself, sturdy and straight:
Precisely this gatepost for this gate.

The poem is itself, the form-in-content:
Exactly these words for what was meant.

The gatepost is rough, distinct and lovable,
Untouched by the purpose that made it possible.

The poem is plain, final, able to please,
Clear of the hungers that made it what it is.

LANDFALL

This is the final aim of every voyage.
Though the young man may run away to sea,
The wind blow dreaming embers into flame,
And under shrapnel spray his body harden,
A tough joy clench his teeth, you will not find
In love of this the motive, though himself
And all the world should think so. Each brief exile
Tunes his blood again to a racy morning
When gulls flicker and squeal around the masts,
The small flags lick the breeze, and the crew
With darkening eyes watch the bows glide home
Into the welcome of the harbour's thighs.

THOMAS KINSELLA

ANOTHER SEPTEMBER

DREAMS fled away, this country bedroom, raw
With the touch of the dawn, wrapped in a minor peace,
Hears through an open window the garden draw
Long pitch black breaths, lay bare its apple trees,
Ripe pear trees, brambles, windfall-sweetened soil,
Exhale rough sweetness against the starry slates.
Nearer the river sleeps St. John's, all toil
Locked fast inside a dream with iron gates.

Domestic Autumn, like an animal
Long used to handling by those countrymen,
Rubs her kind hide against the bedroom wall
Sensing a fragrant child come back again
—Not this half-tolerated consciousness
That plants its grammar in her yielding weather
But that unspeaking daughter, growing less
Familiar where we fell asleep together.

Wakeful moth-wings blunder near a chair,
Toss their light shell at the glass, and go
To inhabit the living starlight. Stranded hair
Stirs on the still linen. It is as though
The black breathing that billows her sleep, her name,
Drugged under judgement, waned and—bearing daggers
And balances—down the lampless darkness they came,
Moving like women: Justice, Truth, such figures.

IN THE RINGWOOD

As I roved out impatiently
Good Friday with my bride
To drink in the rivered Ringwood
The draughty season's pride
A fell dismay held suddenly
Our feet on the green hill-side.

The yellow Spring on Vinegar Hill,
The smile of Slaney water,
The wind in the withered Ringwood,
Grew dark with ancient slaughter.
My love cried out and I beheld her
Change to Sorrow's daughter.

'Ravenhair, what rending
Set those red lips a-shriek,
And dealt those locks in black lament
Like blows on your white cheek,
That in your looks outlandishly
Both woe and fury speak?'

As sharp a lance as the fatal heron
There on the sunken tree
Will strike in the stones of the river
Was the gaze she bent on me.
O her robe into her right hand
She gathered grievously.

'Many times the civil lover
Climbed that pleasant place,
Many times despairing
Died in his love's face,
His spittle turned to vinegar,
Blood in his embrace.

Love that is every miracle
Is torn apart and rent.
The human turns awry
The poles of the firmament.
The fish's bright side is pierced
And good again is spent.

Though every stem on Vinegar Hill
And stone on the Slaney's bed
And every leaf in the living Ringwood
Builds till it is dead
Yet heart and hand, accomplished,
Destroy until they dread.

Dread, a grey devourer,
Stalks in the shade of love.
The dark that dogs our feet
Eats what is sickened of.
The End that stalks Beginning
Hurries home its drove.'

I kissed three times her shivering lips.
I drank their naked chill.
I watched the river shining
Where the heron wiped his bill.
I took my love in my icy arms
In the Spring on Ringwood Hill.

TWO MORALITIES

An Old Atheist Pauses by the Sea

I CHOOSE at random, knowing less and less.
The shambles of the seashore at my feet
Yield a weathered spiral: I confess
—Appalled at how the waves have polished it—
I know that shores are eaten, rocks are split,
Shells ghosted. Something hates unevenness.
The skin turns porcelain, the nerves retreat,
And then the will, and then the consciousness.

Sisters

GRIM Deirdre sought the stony fist, her grief
Capped at last by insult. Pierce's bride,
Sybil Ferriter, fluttered like a leaf
And fell in courtly love to stain the tide.
Each for a murdered husband—hanged in silk
Or speared in harness—threw her body wide,
And offered treachery a bloody milk;
Each cast the other's shadow when she died.

BAGGOT STREET DESERTA

LULLED, at silence, the spent attack.
The will to work is laid aside.
The breaking-cry, the strain of the rack,
Yield, are at peace. The window is wide
On a crawling arch of stars, and the night
Reacts faintly to the mathematic
Passion of a 'cello suite
Plotting the quiet of my attic.
A mile away the river toils
Its buttressed fathoms out to sea;
Tucked in the mountains, many miles
Away from its roaring outcome, a shy
Gasp of waters in the gorse
Is sonnetting origins. Dreamers' heads
Lie mesmerized in Dublin's beds
Flashing with images, Adam's morse.

A cigarette, the moon, a sigh
Of educated boredom, greet
A curlew's lingering threadbare cry
Of common loss. Compassionate,
I add my call of exile, half-
Buried longing, half-serious
Anger and the rueful laugh.
We fly into our risk, the spurious.

Versing, like an exile, makes
A virtuoso of the heart,
Interpreting the old mistakes
And discords in a work of Art
For the One, a private masterpiece
Of doctored recollections. Truth
Concedes, before the dew, its place

In the spray of dried forgettings Youth
Collected when they were a single
Furious undissected bloom.
A voice clarifies when the tingle
Dies out of the nerves of time:
Endure and let the present punish.
Looking backward, all is lost;
The Past becomes a fairy bog
Alive with fancies, double crossed
By pad of owl and hoot of dog,
Where shaven serious-minded men
Appear with lucid theses, after
Which they don the mists again
With trackless, cotton-silly laughter;
Secretly a swollen Burke
Assists a decomposing Hare
To cart a body of good work
With midnight mutterings off somewhere;
The goddess who had light for thighs
Grows feet of dung and takes to bed,
Affronting horror-stricken eyes,
The marsh bird that children dread.

I nonetheless inflict, endure,
Tedium, intracordal hurt,
The sting of memory's quick, the drear
Uprooting, burying, prising apart
Of loves a strident adolescent
Spent in doubt and vanity.
All feel a single stream, impassioned
Now with obsessed honesty,
A tugging scruple that can keep
Clear eyes staring down the mile,
The thousand fathoms, into sleep.

Fingers cold against the sill
Feel, below the stress of flight,

The slow implosion of my pulse
In a wrist with poet's cramp, a tight
Beat tapping out endless calls
Into the dark, as the alien
Garrison in my own blood
Keeps constant contact with the main
Mystery, not to be understood.
Out where imagination arches
Chilly points of light transact
The business of the border-marches
Of the Real, and I—a fact
That may be countered or may not—
Find their privacy complete.

My quarter-inch of cigarette
Goes flaring down to Baggot Street.

THINKING OF MR. D.

A MAN still light of foot, but ageing, took
An hour to drink his glass, his quiet tongue
Danced to such cheerful slander. Yet his look
Was narrowed to the angry ember the young,
If they should notice, would pity as rage barred in
By age, the knot where hope's perspective ends.
(What embers blaze on such a little gin?
What tangled woes fly open till his friends
And peers, the dead, kneel down and help?) But God
And this voluble, black-hatted, scathing elder
Tapping a polished toe, whose sober nod
Mordantly withheld assent, kept wilder
Distance than a step of guttering sighs.
A minding man whose body frays is forced
Into an abstract wrecking humour, his thighs
Gone brittle but his wants not buoyed nor cursed
By the known emotions of the open again.
A joking sorrow clasps him that he should,
Perhaps, find ideal doubt is suddenly won,
And knows his tatters lack the act of blood
To set her spawning; and this man 'beat the wall',
Likely enough—his temper being strong,
The world still mattering—although its fall
Could but distract. He loosened hope like a thong
And new plains opened across the living coal
Time dropped before him, bitten by flaming threads
—Paths that he must people from his soul—
By broken dykes and smouldering watersheds,
A planet he must cross to the dark side
There, in a wonder, to bring forth his fire
And dance on scorching leather. When he died
I saw him twice: once as he used retire,

54

On one last murmured, stabbing little tale,
From the right company, tucking in his scarf,
A barren Dante leaving us for hell;
Then, loping through that image, under wharf-
Lamps that plunged him in and out of light,
A priestlike figure turning, wolfish-slim,
Quickly aside from pain, in a bodily plight,
To note the oiled reflections chime and swim.

A PORTRAIT OF THE ENGINEER

The frock coat and the snowy cuff
Sit well; he handles a bright black hat;
Lips that a moderate span of life
Tautened and drew down are shut.
The boardroom sun dwells on the glass-
And-gold gleam of his picture frame.

Monuments to storm and stress
Endure in foreign lands; at home
Girders lift the lower sky,
Ramps and funnels thunder; all
Born of a dour intensity
That cramped and frowned and drove until
His earthly visions turned to stone
And complex Profit dammed his passion.
Power leaped from son to son
And gathered calm in their succession;
All throve with honour, none fell short
Or raised the fingers to the mouth
When change demanded they take part
In humanism's privy death
To keep that calm unbroken. Now,
To a later eye, the paint reveals
That full logic, plain to see
Alert in his steely spectacles.

And there in a calm within a calm,
Spotless on the heavy baize,
His instrument, a diagram,
Is set to wither mysteries.

Full-fed upon the hushed, glass-smooth
Absorption of its master's desk

A demon rose from the finished task,
Drew intoxicated breath
And flexed its golden strength to pester
The lazy places of the earth;
But when did demon usher master
Lightly from the toils of birth?
His brow on marsh and moor he bent;
Slowly they gave up their hearts
And split the seam of his content.

Another of the brutal arts
Feeds a second demon where
(Ambiguous sympathy gone dumb)
I knock my shoe against a chair
And turn toward sunlight. O should it come
To pass at length that our ghosts met,
We'd match our hatreds in a gaze:
Mine for the flesh his engines ate,
His for the blurred response of a phrase.

WEDDING MORNING

Down the church gravel where the bridal car
  Gleams at the gate among the waifs and strays
And women of Milewater, formal wear
  And Fashion's joker hats wink in the breeze.

Past the hushed progress under sprays of broom
  And choirs of altar lilies, when all eyes
Went brimming with her and the white-lipped groom
  Brought her to kneel beside him. Past the sighs;

Ahead lies the gaiety of her father's hall
  Thrown open to the chatter of champagne,
The poised photographer, the flying veil,
  The motors crowded on the squandered lawn.

Down the bright gravel stroll the families
With Blood, the trader, profiting in their peace.

MIRROR IN FEBRUARY

THE day dawns, with scent of must and rain,
Of opened soil, dark trees, dry bedroom air.
Under the fading lamp, half dressed—my brain
Idling on some compulsive fantasy—
I towel my shaven jaw and stop, and stare,
Riveted by a dark exhausted eye,
A dry downturning mouth.

It seems again that it is time to learn,
In this untiring, crumbling place of growth
To which, for the time being, I return.
Now plainly in the mirror of my soul
I read that I have looked my last on youth
And little more; for they are not made whole
That reach the age of Christ.

Below my window the wakening trees,
Hacked clean for better bearing, stand defaced
Suffering their brute necessities;
And how should the flesh not quail, that span for span
Is mutilated more? In slow distaste
I fold my towel with what grace I can,
Not young, and not renewable, but man.

CHRYSALIDES

Our last free summer we mooned about at odd hours
Pedalling slowly through country towns, stopping to eat
Chocolate and fruit, tracing our vagaries on the map.

At night we watched in the barn, to the lurch of melodeon music,
The crunching boots of countrymen—huge and weightless
As their shadows—twirling and leaping over the yellow concrete.

Sleeping too little or too much, we awoke at noon
And were received with womanly mockery into the kitchen,
Like calves poking our faces in with enormous hunger.

Daily we strapped our saddlebags and went to experience
A tolerance we shall never know again, confusing
For the last time, for example, the licit and the familiar.

Our instincts blurred with change; a strange wakefulness
Sapped our energies and dulled our slow-beating hearts
To the extremes of feeling; insensitive alike

To the unique succession of our youthful midnights,
When by a window ablaze softly with the virgin moon
Dry scones and jugs of milk awaited us in the dark,

Or to lasting horror: a wedding flight of ants
Spawning to its death, a mute perspiration
Glistening like drops of copper, agonized, in our path.

A COUNTRY WALK

SICK of the piercing company of women
I swung the gate shut with a furious sigh,
Rammed trembling hands in pockets and drew in
A breath of river air. A rook's wet wing
Cuffed abruptly upward through the drizzle.

On either hand dead trunks in drapes of creeper,
Strangled softly by horse-mushroom, writhed
In vanished passion, broken down like sponge.
I walked their hushed stations, passion dying,
Each slow footfall a drop of peace returning.

I clapped my gloves. Three cattle turned aside
Their fragrant bodies from a corner gate
And down the sucking chaos of a hedge
Churned land to liquid in their dreamy passage.
Briefly through the beaded grass a path
Led to the holy stillness of a well
And there in the smell of water, stone and leaf
I knelt, baring my hand, and scooped and drank,
Shivering, and inch by inch rejoiced:
Ferocity became intensity.

Or so it seemed as with a lighter step
I turned an ivied corner to confront
The littered fields where summer broke and fled.
Below me, right and left, the valley floor
Tilted, in a silence full of storms;
A ruined aqueduct in delicate rigor
Clenched cat-backed, rooted to one horizon;
A vast asylum reared its potent calm
Up from the other through the sodden air,
Tall towers ochre where the gutters dripped;
A steeple; the long yielding of a railway turn
Through thorn and willow; a town endured its place . . .

Joining the two slopes, blocking an ancient way
With crumbled barracks, castle and brewery
It took the running river, wrinkling and pouring,
Into its blunt embrace. A line of roofs
Fused in veils of rain and steely light
As the dying sun struck it huge glancing blows.
A strand of idle smoke mounted until
An idler current combed it slowly west,
A hook of shadow dividing the still sky . . .
Mated, like a fall of rock, with time,
The place endured its burden: as a froth
Locked in a swirl of turbulence, a shape
That forms and fructifies and dies, a wisp
That hugs the bridge, an omphalos of scraps.

I moved, my glove-backs glistening, over flesh-
And forest-fed earth; till, skirting a marshy field
Where melancholy brambles scored the mud
By the gapped glitter of a speckled ford,
I shuddered with a visual sweet excitement.

Those murmuring shallows made a trampling place
Apt for death-combat, as the tales agree:
There, the day that Christ hung dying, twin
Brothers armed in hate on either side;
The day darkened but they moved to meet
With crossed swords under a dread eclipse
And mingled their bowels at the saga's end.
There the first Normans massacred my fathers,
Then stroked their armoured horses' necks, disposed
In ceremony, sable on green sward.
Twice more the reeds grew red, the stones obscured:
When knot-necked Cromwell and his fervent sword
Dispatched a convent shrieking to their Lover;
And when in peasant fear a rebel host,
Through long retreat grown half hysterical

—Methodical, ludicrous—piked in groups of three
Cromwell's puritan brood, their harmless neighbours,
Forked them half living to the sharp water
And melted into the martyred countryside,
Root eaters, strange as badgers. Pulses calmed;
The racked heroic nerved itself for peace;
Then came harsh winters, motionless waterbirds,
And generations that let welcome fail.

Road and river parted. Now my path
Lay gleaming through the greasy dusk, uphill
Into the final turn. A concrete cross
Low in the ditch grew to the memory
Of one who answered latest the phantom hag,
Tireless Rebellion, when with mouth awry
She hammered at the door, disrupting harvest.
There he bled to death, his line of sight
Blocked by the corner-stone, and did not see
His town ablaze with joy, the grinning foe
Driven in heavy lorries from the field;
And he lay cold in the Hill Cemetery
When freedom burned his comrades' itchy palms,
Too much for flesh and blood, and—armed in hate—
Brother met brother in a modern light.
They turned the bloody corner, knelt and killed,
Who gather still at Easter round his grave,
Our watchful elders. Deep in his crumbled heart
He takes their soil, and chatting they return
To take their town again, that have exchanged
A trenchcoat playground for a gombeen jungle.
Around the corner, in an open square,
I came upon the sombre monuments
That bear their names: MacDonagh & McBride,
Merchants; Connolly's Commercial Arms . . .
Their windows gave me back my stolid self
In attitudes of staring as I paced

Their otherworldly gloom, reflected light
Playing on lens and raincoat stonily.
I turned away. Down the sloping square
A lamp switched on above the urinal;
Across the silent handball alley eyes
That never looked on lover measured mine
Over the Christian Brothers' frosted glass
And turned away. Out of the neighbouring shades
A car plunged soundlessly and disappeared
Pitching downward steeply to the bridge.
I too descended. Naked sycamores,
Assembled dripping near the quay, stood still
And dropped from their combining arms a single
Word upon my upturned face. I trod
The river underfoot: the parapet
Above the central arch received my hands.

Under a darkening and clearing heaven
The hastening river streamed in a slate sheen,
Its face a-swarm. Across the swollen water
(Delicate myriads vanishing in a breath)
Faint ripples winked; a thousand currents broke,
Kissing, dismembering, in threads of foam
Or poured intact over the stony bed
Glass-green and chill; their shallow, shifting world
Slid on in troubled union, forging together
Surfaces that gave and swallowed light;
And grimly the flood divided where it swept
An endless debris through the failing dusk
Under the thudding span beneath my feet.

Venit Hesperus;

In green and golden light; bringing sweet trade.
The inert stirred. Heart and tongue were loosed:
'The waters hurtle through the flooded night . . .'

64

JOHN MONTAGUE

POISONED LANDS

In the countryside one often sees crudely painted signs:
THESE LANDS ARE POISONED. This indicates that meat in-
jected with poison has been laid down to destroy predatory
animals: the practice is not highly regarded.

'FOUR good dogs dead in one night
And a rooster, scaly legs in the air,
Beak in the dust, a terrible sight!'
Behind high weathered walls, his share
Of local lands, the owner skulks
Or leaves in dismal guttering gaps
A trail of broken branches, roots,
Bruised by his mournful rubber boots.

Neighbours sight him as a high hat
Dancing down hedges, a skeletal shape
Night-haloed with whistling bats,
Or silhouetted against cloudy skies,
Coat turned briskly to the nape,
Sou'westered in harsh surmise.

'Children dawdling home from Mass
Chased a bouncing ball and found,
Where he had stood, scorched tufts of grass
Blighted leaves'—and here the sound
Of rodent Gossip sank—'worse by far,
Dark radiance as though a star
Had disintegrated, a clinging stench
Gutting the substances of earth and air.'

At night, like baleful shadowed eyes,
His windows show the way to cars
Igniting the dark like fireflies.
Gusts of song and broken glass
Prelude wild triumphal feasts
Climaxed by sacrifice of beasts.

Privileged, I met him on an evening walk,
Inveigled him into casual weather talk.
'I don't like country people' he said, with a grin.
The winter sunlight halved his mottled chin
And behind, a white notice seemed to swing and say:
'If you too licked grass, you'd be dead today'.

THE WATER CARRIER

Twice daily I carried water from the spring,
Morning before leaving school, and evening;
Balanced as a fulcrum between two buckets.

A bramble rough path ran to the river
Where one stepped carefully across slime-topped stones,
With corners abraded as bleakly white as bones.

At the widening pool (for washing and cattle)
Minute fish flickered as one dipped,
Circling to fill, with rust-tinged water.

The second or enamel bucket was for spring water
Which, after racing through a rushy meadow,
Came bubbling in a broken drain-pipe.

One stood until the bucket brimmed
Inhaling the musty smell of unpicked berries,
That heavy greenness fostered by water.

Recovering the scene, I had hoped to stylize it,
Like the portrait of an Egyptian water-carrier:
Yet halt, entranced by slight but memoried life.

I sometimes come to take the water there,
Not as return or refuge, but some pure thing,
Some living source, half-imagined and half-real

Pulses in the fictive water that I feel.

THE FIRST INVASION OF IRELAND

For Michael Walsh

According to Leabhar Gabhala, The Book of Conquests, the
first invasion of Ireland was by relatives of Noah, just before
the Flood. Refused entry into the Ark, they consulted an idol
which told them to flee to Ireland. There were three men and
fifty-one women in the party and their behaviour had so little
in common with subsequent tradition in Ireland that one must
take the story to be mythological.

FLEEING from threatened flood, they sailed,
Seeking the fair island, without serpent or claw;
From the deck of their hasty windjammer watched
The soft edge of Ireland nearward draw.

A sweet confluence of waters, a trinity of rivers,
Was their first resting place:
They unloaded the women and the sensual idol,
Guiding image of their disgrace.

Division of damsels they did there,
The slender, the tender, the dimpled, the round,
It was the first just bargain in Ireland,
There was enough to go round.

Lightly they lay and pleasured
In the green grass of that guileless place:
Ladhra was the first to die;
He perished of an embrace.

Bith was buried in a stone heap,
Riot of mind, all passion spent.
Fintan fled from the ferocious women
Before he, too, by love was rent.

Great primitive princes of our line
They were the first, with stately freedom
To sleep with women in Ireland:
Soft the eternal bed they lie upon.

On a lonely headland the women assembled,
Chill as worshippers in a nave,
And watched the eastern waters gather
Into a great virile flooding wave.

A FOOTNOTE ON MONASTICISM:
WESTERN PENINSULA

In certain places, still, surprisingly, you come
Upon them, resting like old straw hats set down
Beside the sea, weather-beaten but enduring
Through stubborn Atlantic surge and storm
For a dozen centuries: here the mound
That was the roof has slithered in
And the outlines you can barely trace:
Nor does it matter much since every wilderness
Along this rocky coast retains more signs
In ragged groupings of these cells and caves,
Of where the hermits, fiercely dispossessed ones,
Found refuge among gulls and rocks
The incessant prayer of nearby waves.

See, among darkening rocks he prayed,
Whose body was chastened and absurd,
An earth-bound dragging space in which
His seeking spirit blundered like a bird:
Whose hands, specialized by prayer,
Shone like uplifted chalices,
Nightly proferring the weight of self
To soundless, perfect messengers.

There are times, certainly, looking through a window
At amiable clustered humanity, or scanning
The leaves of some old book, that one might wish
To join their number, start a new and fashionable
Sect beside the Celtic sea, long favourable
To dreams and dreamers; people hurt into solitude
By loss of love; anchorites whose love of God
Was selfishly alone, a matter so great

That only to stone could they whisper it:
Breaking the obstinate structure of flesh
With routine of vigil and fast,
Till water-cress stirred on the palate
Like the movement of a ghost.

In ceaseless labour of the spirit,
Isolate, unblessed;
Until quietude of the senses
Announces presence of a guest;
Desolation final,
Rock within and rock without
Till from the stubborn rock of the heart,
The purifying waters spurt.

RECONSTRUCTION

On the building lot at Vaugirard
Most of the workers are Algerian.
They begin early, a pneumatic drill
Rivetting the dawn at seven o'clock;
Bang of hammers, creak of windlass,
Clash of iron supports.

But, if you watch closely,
Always the same amount gets done—
Enough but not too much.
They flirt with girls at a window,
Flash mirror-messages,
Chant endless exile songs.

And then the overseers come,
Middle-class Frenchmen, neatly dressed, serious.
If 'the quality of the affection' is important,
So also is 'the quality of disaffection',
Saying: 'I work as I am paid'
Or, 'These are not *our* houses!'

It reminds me of a Dublin barge
Passing through a lock on the Grand Canal.
It took four men, a donkey,
And twenty onlookers, half a morning.
While the water rose they smoked,
Discussed horses, or just chewed grass.

Today, in Paris, whole areas change,
The horizon heavy with cranes.
When a working-class district goes residential
So also go colourful markets, cheap restaurants.
Only some concierges may remain,
Encased in new concrete like fossils.

PARIS: APRIL 1961

When news of the Algerian Putsch came
I saw fright in some faces
But the traffic went on, undismayed,
And when I asked the woman at the kiosk
'Il y a quelque chose de nouveau?'
She said, 'C'est tout dans le journal'.
She probably said that before the fall of France.

The man and woman on the seventh floor
Quarrelled bitterly over something, all day,
While I sat at a table reading and working,
And watched the rain spread over Paris.
Later, however, one saw the real thing,
Shermans in the Concorde,
Under the candled chestnuts of the Cours la Reine,

And Malraux's pale face at a window,
Comically passionate, a period revived.
Distress is nearly always somewhere else,
And even when it isn't, it is hard
To know what is happening, how to help.
That Sunday there was a rainbow over the city.
Portents are not always as auspicious.

THE COUNTRY FIDDLER

My uncle played the fiddle—more elegantly, the violin—
A favourite at barn and cross-roads dance,
He knew *The Sailor's Bonnet* and *The Fowling Piece.*

Bachelor head of a house full of sisters,
Runner of poor racehorses, spendthrift;
He left for a New World in an old disgrace.

He left his fiddle in the rafters
When he sailed, never played afterwards:
A rural art irrelevant in the harshness of Brooklyn.

A heavily-built man, tranquil-eyed as an ox,
He ran a wild speakeasy, and died of it.
During the depression many dossed in his cellar.

I attended his funeral, in the Church of the Redemption,
Then, unexpected successor, reversed time
To return where he had been born.

During my schooldays the fiddle rusted,
(The bridge fell away, the catgut snapped)
Reduced to a plaything stinking of stale rosin.

The country people asked if I also had music
(All the family had had) but the fiddle was in pieces
And the rafters remade, before I discovered my craft.

To fiddle means, in country terms, to play the violin;
More modishly now, to wangle money, or idle one's time:
He tried all three: I am forced to the same.

Twenty years afterwards, I saw the church again,
And promised to remember my burly godfather
And his rural craft, after this fashion:

So succession passes, through strangest hands.

A ROYAL VISIT

Tara, though she be desolate today,
Once was the habitation of heroes . . .
                    from *The Book of Leinster*

I

THE deep cooing of doves
As we move towards the earthen fort
Is a subtly insidious music
Designed to exhort:
Axehead of the intellect washed
In hovering fragrance of hawthorn,
The primary colours of a summer morning.

II

This martial extravagance of mounds
Cannot be approached simply:
Through ritual sagas it resounds
With din of war and love.
Devious virgins and fisty men
Gesturing against the sky,
Invoke the seasonal crucifixion.

III

Gaelic Acropolis or smoky hovel?
In the enormous osiered banquet hall,
The sotted bards rehearse
A genealogical glory:
Stately assonance of verse
Petrifies wolf-skinned warriors
In galleries of race.

77

IV

Who longs for subtler singing,
Muted vocal of the dove,
Seeks erotic terror ringing
Over stony beds of love:
Couple and landscape blended,
Till beneath the hunchback mountain
Rears the fated boar of death.

V

A battle of miracles
Proves the Christian dispensation,
Druidic snow turning
To merciful Christian rain.
Christ is the greater magician.
No more the phallic stone
Screams for its ritual king.

VI

A mournful St. Patrick surveys
This provincial magnificence;
He sees what twitching sentries saw
When five regal roads
Across a landscape drew:
The central lands of Meath dissolve
Into royal planes of blue.

WILD SPORTS OF THE WEST

THE landlord's coat is tulip red,
A beacon on the wine-dark moor;
He turns his well-bred foreign devil's face,
While his bailiff trots before.

His furious hooves drum fire from stone,
A beautiful sight when gone;
Contemplation holds the noble horseman
In his high mould of bone.

Not so beautiful the bandy bailiff,
Churlish servant of an alien will:
Behind the hedge a maddened peasant
Poises his shotgun for the kill.

Evening brings the huntsman home,
Blood of pheasants in a bag:
Beside a turfrick the cackling peasant
Cleanses his ancient weapon with a rag.

The fox, evicted from the thicket,
Evades with grace the snuffling hounds:
But a transplanted bailiff, in a feudal paradise,
Patrols for God His private grounds.

OLD MYTHOLOGIES

AND now, at last, all proud deeds done,
Mouths dust-stopped, dark they embrace
Suitably disposed, as urns, underground.
Cattle munching soft spring grass
—Epicures of shamrock and the four-leafed clover—
Hear a whimper of ancient weapons,
As a whole dormitory of heroes turn over,
Regretting their butchers' days.
This valley cradles their archaic madness
As once, on an impossibly epic morning,
It upheld their savage stride:
To bagpiped battle marching,
Wolfhounds, lean as models,
At their urgent heels.

WOODTOWN MANOR

For Morris Graves

I

HERE the delicate dance of silence,
The quick step of the robin,
The sudden skittering rush of the wren:
Minute essences move in and out of creation
Until the skin of soundlessness forms again.

Part order, part wilderness,
Water creates its cadenced illusion
Of glaucous, fluent growth;
Fins raised, as in a waking dream,
Bright fish probe their painted stream.

Imaginary animals harbour here:
The young fox coiled in its covert,
Bright-eyed and mean, the baby bird:
The heron, like a radiant initial,
Illuminating the gospel of the absurd.

And all the menagerie of the living marvellous:
Stone shape of toad,
Flicker of insect life,
Shift of wind touched grass
As though a beneficent spirit stirred.

II

Twin deities hover in Irish air
Reconciling poles of east and west;
The detached and sensual Indian God,
Franciscan dream of gentleness:
Gravity of Georgian manor
Approves, with classic stare,
Their dual discipline of tenderness.

III

Courtesy of evening light brings
Such perspectives to a spatial blaze:
Pattern of trees and variegated wall
Kindles to a brief amaze;
Water spreads ring on widening ring
Of silence, until images commingle
In a darkening tide of wings.

AUSCHWITZ, MON AMOUR

AUSCHWITZ, mon amour!
A welcoming party of almost shades
Met us at the cinema door
Clicking what remained of their heels.

From nests of bodies like hatching eggs
Flickered insectlike hands and legs
And rose an ululation, terrible, shy,
Like children conjugating the verb 'to die'.

One clamoured mutely of love
From a mouth like a burned glove;
Others upheld hands bleak as begging bowls
Claiming the small change of our souls.

Some smiled at us as protectors.
Can these bones live?
Our parochial brand of innocence
Was all we had to give.

To be always at the periphery of incident
Gave my childhood its Irish dimension; drama of unevent:
Yet doves of mercy, as doves of air,
Can tumble here as anywhere.

It takes a decade and a half, it seems,
Even to comprehend one's dreams:
Continual operation on the body of the past
Brings final meaning to its birth at last.

That long dead Sunday in Armagh
I learned one meaning of total war
And went home to my Christian school
And kicked a football through the air.

LIKE DOLMENS ROUND MY CHILDHOOD, THE OLD PEOPLE

Like Dolmens round my childhood, the old people.

I

JAMIE MacCRYSTAL sang to himself,
A broken song without tune, without words;
He tipped me a penny every pension day,
Fed kindly crusts to winter birds.
When he died, his cottage was robbed,
Mattress and money box torn and searched,
Only the corpse they didn't disturb.

II

Maggie Owens was surrounded by animals,
A mongrel bitch and shivering pups,
Even in her bedroom a she-goat cried.
She was a well of gossip defiled,
Fanged chronicler of a whole countryside;
Reputed a witch, all I could find
Was her ravening need to deride.

III

The Nialls lived along a mountain lane
Where heather bells bloomed, clumps of foxglove.
All were blind, with Blind Pension and Wireless,
Dead eyes serpent-flicked as one entered
To shelter from a downpour of mountain rain.
Crickets chirped under the rocking hearthstone
Until the muddy sun shone out again.

Mary Moore lived in a crumbling gatehouse,
Famous as Pisa for its leaning gable.
Bag apron and boots, she tramped the fields
Driving lean cattle from a miry stable.
A by-word for fierceness, she fell asleep
Over love stories, Red Star and Red Circle,
Dreamed of gypsy love rites, by firelight sealed.

V

Wild Billy Harbison married a Catholic servant girl
When all his Loyal family passed on:
We danced round him shouting 'To Hell with King Billy',
And dodged from the arc of his flailing blackthorn.
Forsaken by both creeds, he showed little concern
Until the Orange drums banged past in the summer
And bowler and sash aggressively shone.

Curate and doctor trudged to attend them,
Through knee-deep snow, through summer heat,
From main road to lane to broken path,
Gulping the mountain air with painful breath.
Sometimes they were found by neighbours,
Silent keepers of a smokeless hearth,
Suddenly cast in the mould of death.

Ancient Ireland, indeed! I was reared by her bedside,
The rune and the chant, evil eye and averted head,
Formorian fierceness of family and local feud.
Gaunt figures of fear and of friendliness,
For years they trespassed on my dreams,
Until once, in a standing circle of stones,
I felt their shadows pass

Into that dark permanence of ancient forms.

RICHARD MURPHY

SAILING TO AN ISLAND

THE boom above my knees lifts, and the boat
Drops, and the surge departs, departs, my cheek
Kissed and rejected, kissed, as the gaff sways
A tangent, cuts the infinite sky to red
Maps, and the mast draws eight and eight across
Measureless blue, the boatmen sing or sleep.

We point all day for our chosen island,
Clare, with its crags purpled by legend:
There under castles the hot O'Malleys,
Daughters of Granuaile, the pirate queen
Who boarded a Turk with a blunderbuss,
Comb red hair and assemble cattle.
Across the shelved Atlantic groundswell
Plumbed by the sun's kingfisher rod,
We sail to locate in sea, earth and stone
The myth of a shrewd and brutal swordswoman
Who piously endowed an abbey.
Seven hours we try against wind and tide,
Tack and return, making no headway.
The north wind sticks like a gag in our teeth.

Encased in a mirage, steam on the water,
Loosely we coast where hideous rocks jag
An acropolis of cormorants, an extinct
Volcano where spiders spin, a purgatory
Guarded by hags and bristled with breakers.

The breeze as we plunge slowly stiffens:
There are hills of sea between us and land,
Between our hopes and the island harbour.
A child vomits. The boat veers and bucks.

There is no refuge on the gannet's cliff.
We are far, far out: the hull is rotten,
The spars are splitting, the rigging is frayed,
And our helmsman laughs uncautiously.
What of those who must earn their living
On the ribald face of a mad mistress?
We in holiday fashion know
This is the boat that belched its crew
Dead on the shingle in the Cleggan disaster.

Now she dips, and the sail hits the water.
She hoves to a squall; is struck; and shudders.
Someone is shouting. The boom, weak as scissors,
Has snapped. The boatman is praying.
Orders thunder and canvas cannonades.
She smothers in spray. We still have a mast;
The oar makes a boom. I am told to cut
Cords out of fishing-lines, fasten the jib.
Ropes lash my cheeks. Ease! Ease at last:
She swings to leeward, we can safely run.
Washed over rails our Clare Island dreams,
With storm behind us we straddle the wakeful
Waters that draw us headfast to Inishbofin.

The bows rock as she overtakes the surge.
We neither sleep nor sing nor talk,
But look to the land where the men are mowing.
What will the islanders think of our folly?

The whispering spontaneous reception committee
Nods and smokes by the calm jetty.
Am I jealous of these courteous fishermen
Who hand us ashore, for knowing the sea
Intimately, for respecting the storm
That took nine of their men on one bad night
And five from Rossadillisk in this very boat?

Their harbour is sheltered. They are slow to tell
The story again. There is local pride
In their home-built ships.
We are advised to return next day by the mail.

But tonight we stay, drinking with people
Happy in the monotony of boats,
Bringing the catch to the Cleggan market,
Cultivating fields, or retiring from America
With enough to soak till morning or old age.

The bench below my knees lifts, and the floor
Drops, and the words depart, depart, with faces
Blurred by the smoke. An old man grips my arm,
His shot eyes twitch, quietly dissatisfied.
He has lost his watch, an American gold
From Boston gas-works. He treats the company
To the secretive surge, the sea of his sadness.
I slip outside, fall among stones and nettles,
Crackling dry twigs on an elder tree,
While an accordion drones above the hill.

Later, I reach a room, where the moon stares
Cob-webbed through the window. The tide has ebbed,
Boats are careened in the harbour. Here is a bed.

THE LAST GALWAY HOOKER

The *Ave Maria*, launched in 1922, was the last of the old sailing hookers built in Galway. She is one of a few that still survive. The boatwright is described as 'tasty' in the Galway sense of a craftsman who does both skilled and polished work. The trade name 'Ailsa Craig' belongs to a popular make of diesel engine. 'Spillets' (also called 'spillers') are long fishing-lines with a hundred or more hooks, joined together to make miles of line, and set on the bottom for cod, ling, and flat fish. 'Trammels' are nets used locally for catching baits for the spillets and lobster pots.

Metrical note. The typical line has four stresses (of varying weight) which fall usually into two groups of two stresses each. The opening lines set the pattern, with the words containing the stresses italicized:

> Where the *Corrib river* | *chops* through the *Claddagh*
> To *sink* in the *tide-race* | its *rattling chain*
> The *boatwright's hammer* | *chipped* across the *water*

WHERE the Corrib river chops through the Claddagh
To sink in the tide-race its rattling chain
The boatwright's hammer chipped across the water

Ribbing this hooker, while a reckless gun
Shook the limestone quay-wall, after the Treaty
Had brought civil war to this fisherman's town.

That 'tasty' carpenter from Connemara, Cloherty,
Helped by his daughter, had half-planked the hull
In his eightieth year, when at work he died,

And she did the fastening, and caulked her well,
The last boat completed with old Galway lines.
Several seasons at the drift-nets she paid

In those boom-years, working by night in channels
With trammel and spillet and an island crew,
Tea-stew on turf in the pipe-black forecastle,

Songs of disasters wailed on the quay
When the tilt of the water heaves the whole shore.
'She was lucky always the *Ave Maria*',

With her brown barked sails, and her hull black tar,
Her forest of oak ribs and the larchwood planks,
The cavern-smelling hold bulked with costly gear,

Fastest in the race to the gull-marked banks,
What harbour she hived in, there she was queen
And her crew could afford to stand strangers drinks,

Till the buyers failed in nineteen twenty-nine,
When the cheapest of fish could find no market,
Were dumped overboard, the price down to nothing,

Until to her leisure a fisher priest walked
By the hungry dockside, full of her name,
Who made a cash offer, and the owners took it.

Then like a girl given money and a home
With no work but pleasure for her man to perform
She changed into white sails, her hold made room

For hammocks and kettles, the touch and perfume
Of priestly hands. So now she's a yacht
With pitch-pine spars and Italian hemp ropes,

Smooth-running ash-blocks expensively bought
From chandlers in Dublin, two men get jobs
Copper-painting her keel and linseeding her throat,

While at weekends, nephews and nieces in mobs
Go sailing on picnics to the hermit islands,
Come home flushed with health having hooked a few dabs.

Munich, submarines, and the war's demands
Of workers to feed invaded that party
Like fumes of the diesel the dope of her sails,

When the Canon went east into limed sheep-lands
From the stone and reed patches of lobstermen
Having sold her to one on Cleggan Quay,

Who was best of the boatsmen from Inishbofin,
She his best buy. He shortened the mast, installed
A new 'Ailsa Craig', made a hold of her cabin,

Poured over the deck thick tar slightly boiled;
Every fortnight he drained the sump in the bilge
'To preserve the timbers'. All she could do, fulfilled.

The sea, good to gamblers, let him indulge
His fear when she rose winding her green shawl
And his pride when she lay calm under his pillage:

And he never married, was this hooker's lover,
Always ill-at-ease in houses or on hills,
Waiting for weather, or mending broken trawls:

Bothered by women no more than by the moon,
Not concerned with money beyond the bare need,
In this boat's bows he sheathed his life's harpoon.

A neap-tide of work, then a spring of liquor
Were the tides that alternately pulled his soul,
Now on a pitching deck with nets to hand-haul,

Then passing Sunday propped against a barrel
Winding among words like a sly helmsman
Till stories gather around him in a shoal.

She was Latin blessed, holy water shaken
From a small whiskey bottle by a surpliced priest,
Madonnas wafered on every bulkhead,

Oil-grimed by the diesel, and her luck lasted
Those twenty-one years of skill buoyed by prayers,
Strength forged by dread from his drowned ancestors.

She made him money, and again he lost it
In the fisherman's fiction of turning farmer:
The cost of timber and engine spares increased,

Till a phantom hurt him, ribs on a shore,
A hull each tide rattles that will never fish,
Sunk back in the sand, a story finished.

We met here last summer, nineteen fifty-nine,
Far from the missiles, the moon-shots, the money,
And we drank looking out on the island quay,

When his crew were in London drilling a motorway.
Old age had smoothed his barnacled will
And with wild songs he sold me the *Ave Maria*.

Then he was alone, stunned like a widower—
Relics and rowlocks pronging from the wall,
A pot of boiling garments, winter everywhere,

Especially in his bones, watching things fall,
Hooks of three-mile spillets, trammels at the foot
Of the unused double-bed—his mind threaded with all

The marline of his days twined within that boat,
His muscles' own shackles then staying the storm
Which now snap to bits like frayed thread.

So I chose to renew her, to rebuild, to prolong
For a while the spliced yards of yesterday.
Carpenters were enrolled, the ballast and the dung

Of cattle he'd carried lifted from the hold,
The engine removed, and the stale bilge scoured.
De Valera's daughter hoisted the Irish flag

At her freshly adzed mast this Shrove Tuesday,
Stepped while afloat between the tackle of the *Topaz*
And the *St. John*, by Bofin's best boatsmen,

All old as himself. Her skilful sailmaker,
Her inherited boatwright, her dream-tacking steersman
Picked up the tools of their interrupted work,

And in memory's hands this hooker was restored.
Old men my instructors, and with all new gear
May I handle her well down tomorrow's sea-road.

From THE CLEGGAN DISASTER

(This is the concluding section of a narrative poem about the disaster in 1927 off the west of Ireland, when twenty-five fishermen were lost in a great storm.)

YEARS LATER

WHOSE is that hulk on the shingle
The boatwright's son repairs
Though she has not been fishing
For thirty-four years
Since she rode the disaster?
The oars were turned into rafters
For a roof stripped by a gale.
Moss has grown on her keel.

Where are the red-haired women
Chattering along the piers
Who gutted millions of mackerel
And baited the spillet hooks
With mussels and lug-worms?
All the hurtful hours
Thinking the boats were coming
They hold against those years.

Where are the barefoot children
With brown toes in the ashes
Who went to the well for water,
Picked winkles on the beach
And gathered sea-rods in winter?
The lime is green on the stone
Which they once kept white-washed.
In summer nettles return.

Where are the dances in houses
With porter and cakes in the room,
The reddled faces of fiddlers
Sawing out jigs and reels,
The flickering eyes of neighbours?
The thatch which was neatly bordered
By a fringe of sea-stones
Has now caved in.

Why does she stand at the curtains
Combing her seal-grey hair
And uttering bitter opinions
On land-work and sea-fear,
Drownings and famines?
When will her son say,
'Forget about the disaster,
We're mounting nets today!'

GIRL AT THE SEASIDE

I LEAN on a lighthouse rock
Where the seagowns flow,
A trawler slips from the dock
Sailing years ago.

Wine, tobacco and seamen
Cloud the green air,
A head of snakes in the rain
Talks away desire.

A sailor kisses me
Tasting of mackerel,
I analyse misery
Till mass bells peal.

I wait for clogs on the cobbles,
Dead feet at night,
Only a tempest blows
Darkness on sealight.

I've argued myself here
To the blue cliff-tops:
I'll drop through the sea-air
Till everything stops.

THE NETTING

You have netted this night
From the sea a vase
Which once we carried
At the festivals
In Phaestos where
A young prince ruled
And a stone leopard
Crouched on the walls
Guarding those granaries
And the golden bulls.

Until one April hour's
Earthquake of defeat
By galleys that grooved
Our unwary waters,
When the oil of peace
Blazed in every cruse,
Home became for us
The weltering sea
And language a hiss
In the wood of oars.

Then through gorges on the run
Alone I crawled
To a scorpion plain
Dry with poppies
To bury the stolen
Treasure of cities,
And I passed those years
Dumb below pines
A slave to the pleasures
Of the land of quince.

By the nets of your grace
My heart was hauled
From the heavy mud,
And tonight we sailed
To this island garden
Flaming with asphodel,
Moonlight raking
The early corn,
While the spades rang
On our lost foundation.

I have learnt to restore
From dust each room
The earthquakes lowered
In that doomed spring,
To piece beyond the fire
The cypress court
With gryphons basking,
Wander in the snow
Of almonds before
Those petals were wasting.

You have taken this night
Years of grievance
From the silted heart
And broken the script
Into household language,
You have cut into me
That gypsum field
Happy with harvesters
Fluting the sky
With sheaves on their shoulders.

THE PHILOSOPHER AND THE BIRDS

(In memory of Wittgenstein at Rossroe)

A SOLITARY invalid in a fuchsia garden
Where time's rain eroded the root since Eden,
He became for a tenebrous epoch the stone.

Here wisdom surrendered the don's gown
Choosing, for Cambridge, two deck chairs,
A kitchen table, undiluted sun.

He clipped with February shears the dead
Metaphysical foliage. Old, in fieldfares
Fantasies rebelled though annihilated.

He was haunted by gulls beyond omega shade,
His nerve tormented by terrified knots
In pin-feathered flesh. But all folly repeats

Is worth one snared robin his fingers untied.
He broke prisons, beginning with words,
And at last tamed, by talking, wild birds.

Through accident of place, now by belief
I follow his love which bird-handled thoughts
To grasp growth's terror or death's leaf.

He last on this savage promontory shored
His logical weapon. Genius stirred
A soaring intolerance to teach a blackbird.

So before alpha you may still hear sing
In the leaf-dark dusk some descended young
Who exalt the evening to a wordless song.

His wisdom widens: he becomes worlds
Where thoughts are wings. But at Rossroe hordes
Of village cats have massacred his birds.

THE POET ON THE ISLAND

(To Theodore Roethke)

On a wet night, laden with books for luggage,
And stumbling under the burden of himself,
He reached the pier, looking for a refuge.

Darkly he crossed to the island six miles off:
The engine pulsed, the sails invented rhythm,
While the sea expanded and the rain drummed softly.

Safety on water, he rocked with a new theme:
And in the warmth of his mind's greenhouse bloomed
A poem as graceful as a chrysanthemum.

His forehead, a Prussian helmet, moody, domed,
Relaxed in the sun: a lyric was his lance.
To be loved by the people, he, a stranger, hummed

In the herring-store on Sunday crammed with drunks
Ballads of bawdry with a speakeasy stress.
Yet lonely they left him, 'one of the Yanks'.

The children understood. This was not madness.
How many orphans had he fathered in words
Robust and cunning, but never heartless.

He watched the harbour scouted by sea-birds:
His fate was like fish under poetry's beaks:
Words began weirdly to take off inwards.

Time that they calendar in seasons not in clocks,
In gardens dug over and houses roofed,
Was to him a see-saw of joys and shocks,

Where his body withered but his style improved.
A storm shot up, his glass cracked in a gale:
An abstract thunder of darkness deafened

The listeners he'd once given roses, now hail.
He'd burst the lyric barrier: logic ended.
Doctors were called, and he agreed to sail.

THE PROGRESS OF A PAINTER

Success had not reached his untutored brush
Which wavered in the greys of wintry granite,
Fondly churning the foam of a mountain gulch
While a few rowan berries rained upon it.

He lived in a shack almost on the snow-line
Sleeping on straw. A lantern swung from the rafters.
Squalls from the mine-heaps bellowed in the glen.
He dreamt of icebergs and the flight of eiders.

In loneliness to hatch out his young works
He'd left the seaport's gannet colony,
Their saffron mating-hoods with pirate beaks
And wings of dazzling whiteness tipped with envy.

He painted single birds, but not the flocks:
He drew the great unsociable black-backed gull
Feathered with predatory elegance
Eating a heron's brains beside a pool.

He failed with people: the tanned shepherd's head
Looked like a hawthorn in his gardening hands.
But when sad thrushes on the spikes of greed
Chanted, it was an epiphany of friends.

Upon a penal rock in the holy lake
A cormorant stood, spreading its wings to dry
In the pinewood breeze, and he, the hermit's relic,
Punished his heart to please his lordly eye.

He'd come with egg-shells of extinct religion
Sucked of their yolk, the treasure of his pocket,
A tiger's tooth from a temple in Ceylon,
Flute-players on a soapstone vase from Crete.

Barred aviaries of birds that never flew
But hopped around his hierophantic mind
With lacquered plumes gaudier than pheasants grow,
Escaped at last through water, sedge and wind.

Sometimes he wormed the river for a trout
And waded through brown weedy indolence,
But never a lazy fish would seize the bait
Unless another fish appeared to pounce.

He set a match to the gorse on the high fox-cover,
Subsoiled, harrowed and sowed deep-rooting herbs,
Coxfoot and chicory and wild white clover,
Seeds of all shades the summer sun disturbs.

He pitched his art in a love-suit with the landscape
Which fields of tillage helped to consummate.
To paint a shepherd need he have kept sheep?
His crops of barley were a veiled self-portrait.

Had there been time, he would have planted trees:
But as with a deathly wail the northern diver
Solemnly rises over the requiem seas
And leaves the nesting dunes for the open water,

He had to climb, from the fullness of his leys,
To a new detachment, such as the unknown skies
Offer the airman with his intricate knowledge
How to propel the last machine through space.

EPITAPH ON A FIR-TREE

SHE grew ninety years through sombre winter,
Rhododendron summer of midges and rain,
In a beechwood scarred by the auctioneer,

Till a March evening, the garden work done,
It seemed her long life had been completed,
No further growth, no gaiety could remain.

At a wedding breakfast bridesmaids planted
With trowel and gloves this imported fir.
How soon, measured by trees, the party ended.

Arbour and crinoline have gone under
The laurel, gazebos under the yews:
Wood for wood, we have little to compare.

We think no more of granite steps and pews,
Or an officer patched with a crude trepan
Who fought in Rangoon for these quiet acres.

Axes and saws now convert the evergreen
Imperial shadows into deal boards,
And let the sun enter our house again.

Quickly we'll spend the rings that she hoarded
In her gross girth. The evening is ours.
Those delicate girls who earthed her up are faded.

Except for daffodils, the ground is bare:
We two are left. They walked through pergolas
And planted well, so that we might do better.

THE WOMAN OF THE HOUSE

In memory of my grandmother Lucy Mary Ormsby
whose home was in the west of Ireland

1873–1958

On a patrician evening in Ireland
I was born in the guest-room: she delivered me.
May I deliver her from the cold hand
Where now she lies, with a brief elegy?

It was her house where we spent holidays,
With candles to bed, and ghostly stories:
In the lake of her heart we were islands
Where the wild asses galloped in the wind.

Her mind was a vague and log-warmed yarn
Spun between sleep and acts of kindliness:
She fed our feelings as dew feeds the grass
On April nights, and our mornings were green:

And those happy days, when in spite of rain
We'd motor west where the salmon-boats tossed,
She would sketch on the pier among the pots
Waves in a sunset, or the rising moon.

Indian-meal porridge and brown soda-bread,
Boiled eggs and buttermilk, honey from gorse,
Far more than we wanted she always offered,
In a heart-surfeit—she ate little herself.

Mistress of mossy acres and unpaid rent,
She crossed the walls on foot to feed the sick:
Though frugal cousins frowned on all she spent
People had faith in her healing talent.

She bandaged the wounds that poverty caused
In the house that famine labourers built,
Gave her hands to cure impossible wrong
In a useless way, and was loved for it.

Hers were the fruits of a family tree:
A china clock, the Church's calendar,
Gardeners polite, governesses plenty,
And incomes waiting to be married for.

How the feckless fun would flicker her face
Reading our future by cards at the fire,
Rings and elopements, love-letters, old lace,
A signet of jokes to seal our desire.

'It was sad about Maud, poor Maud!' she'd sigh
To think of the friend she lured and teased
Till she married the butler. 'Starved to death,
No service either by padre or priest.'

Cholera raged in the Residency:
'They kept my uncle alive on port.'
Which saved him to slaughter a few sepoys
And retire to Galway in search of sport.

The pistol that lost an ancestor's duel,
The hoof of the horse that carried him home
To be stretched on chairs in the drawing-room,
Hung by the Rangoon prints and the Crimean medal.

Lever and Lover, Somerville and Ross
Have fed the same worm as Blackstone and Gibbon,
The mildew has spotted *Clarissa*'s spine
And soiled the *Despatches of Wellington*.

Beside her bed lay an old bible that
Her Colonel Rector husband used to read,
And a new *Writers' and Artists' Year-book*
To bring a never-printed girlhood back.

The undeveloped thoughts died in her head,
But from her heart, through the people she loved,
Images spread, and intuitions lived,
More than the mere sense of what she said.

At last, her warmth made ashes of the trees
Ancestors planted, and she was removed
To hospital, to die there, certified.
Her house, but not her kindness, has found heirs.

Compulsory comforts penned her limping soul:
With all she uttered they smiled and agreed.
When she summoned the chauffeur, no one obeyed,
But a chrome hearse was ready for nightfall.

'Order the car for nine o'clock tonight!
I must get back, get back. They're expecting me.
I'll bring the spiced beef and the nuts and fruit.
Sister, I like you. Do come home with me!

'The house in flames and nothing is insured!
Send for the doctor, let the horses go.
The dogs are barking again. Has the cow
Calved in the night? What is that great singed bird?

'I don't know who you are, but you've kind eyes.
My children are abroad and I'm alone.
They left me in this gaol. You all tell lies.
You're not my people. My people have gone.'

Now she's spent everything: the golden waste
Is washed away, silent her heart's hammer.
The children overseas no longer need her,
They are like aftergrass to her harvest.

People she loved were those who worked the land
Whom the land satisfied more than wisdom:
They've gone, a tractor ploughs where horses strained,
Sometimes sheep occupy their roofless room.

Through our inheritance all things have come,
The form, the means, all by our family:
The good of being alive was given through them,
We ourselves limit that legacy.

The bards in their beds once beat out ballads
Under leaky thatch listening to sea-birds,
But she in the long ascendancy of rain
Served biscuits on a tray with ginger wine.

Time can never relax like this again,
She in her phaeton looking for folklore,
He writing sermons in the library
Till lunch, then fishing all the afternoon.

On a wet winter evening in Ireland
I let go her hand, and we buried her
In the family earth beside her husband.
Only to think of her, now warms my mind.

RICHARD WEBER

LADY AND GENTLEMAN

OF himself to think this: she does not
Know my meaning nor ever will,
Though the leaves like late butterflies
Twist and turn, falter and fall
In the outside racing, interlacing winds.

And she, seeing this, that and that
Other yet sees nothing of these,
Is contemplative in her conducted contempt
Of this contact of the customary, this always
And always to be expected, the look of love.

And all else but herself: herself she sees
And is pleased and displeased by turns
Of her thought, of her head also.
One can see it in the constant,
Constrained movements of her denying head.

So fine a thing this is, balanced like held
Breath between beauty and plainness.
When the eyes hold one, they hold so fast
It is only by one's arrival at their awaiting
Uninterest that one releases, is released, dropped.

To fall as one can in one's napkin,
Like a soupdrop, desiring not to be noticed.
Nevertheless, nerveless, one looks up to see
If she can see. Then what joy that she sees,
What, you? No, she watches not you, not

Even now the appearance of you. What, then?
He has seen already that in that steady
Amazing gaze of her eyes there is merely
Awareness of self, herself, and maybe not
Only that, but of whole hordes of women

Who have come together in this one woman.
It is not enough, he knows, but it is more
Than one man, representing only himself,
Can bear, which is why shortly he must dab
At his dismayed mouth with his already raised napkin.

PORTRAIT OF A STATESMAN

THE pedestrian armies stand opposed,
Eyeing each other's eyes across the road.
The gloved hand of law being lowered
They rush across the crossing. Stirred
They fight, but only to find a position
In the crowds. He sees, while massed bands
Of horns and bells play on and on,
The paths of countless cities changing hands.

This face, with its wall-like forehead,
Its pitted eyes, its rough and florid
Cheeks, inclines to wear a too imperious
Look, or so the people say, serious
As ever in their demand that none
Shall claim the time, who cannot see
Whose fall is thus presaged: his own,
The state's, their own; or all three.

HAMPSTEAD HEATH

SUN-SOOTHED, the evening sighs, stretches
Its arms wide behind the lovers' backs,
Declares its air of timelessness and time
Recalled, how many Springs began this way,
The gardens feathery with flowers and foliage,
The scents mixing of earth and memory's blooms.

Heeltip-taps along the pavement strike
Like a blind man's stick picking out
The audible signs of the invisible world
As the lovers walk, blind to their blundering,
Staring intent in the trance of belief of love,
Fingers interlaced, gay gazes interlocked.

The unamazed evening muddies its colours,
Flowers begin to close, breezes to tease.
Trees shake their heads and dark runs its ink
Across the sky as evening prepares for night,
Merging its moods and colours, stretching
Further its far-reaching hand across the scene.

As in a picture, the lovers break away
To pieces of indistinct, distant colour
Along the hilled and tilted Hampstead streets.
While Spring still breathes and whispers
Its promises into the breeze, street-lamps'
Blink banishes the vanished lovers home.

SHAW HOUSE

Just a few properties and props of the heart,
This earth I know and know I love,
Tree and beast and house and meadow.
Out of such a peace or a pride can start,
Where a walking man trails his shadow
In the light like day from that moon above.

One time relations raced at tennis there,
Faced up to youth's skilled suddenness
And lost the ball among those bushes which
Once when young I crouched in, hoping to stare
The house awake from the Shadow Witch,
And saw in sudden lamplight a lady in an age-old dress.

Always imagination asks for the full significance,
From even such memories, desired and seen.
As ever I pray that this may come
Till all is ordered by that changeling chance
Of the poet's faith, the theme's momentum;
Yet what is this but a convent on a public green?

Now the house is a day-school run by nuns
I, if I were old, and though no senator,
Could add a piece to that theme of Yeats
And show the change and fall when guns
Are put away and power becomes the State's.
Not yet full-grown, I must let the nuns explore.

And perhaps, as was said, they will do no harm,
And true that they do only what their duty is.
Here a hundred girls have more right than a family
Which no longer needs its home; while to farm
Out children in the Lord is finer to see
Than lands stuck about with trees and bushes.

The right is theirs by purchase and by faith.
Why I disturb such present peace is hard to show.
I give in answer only the right and claim
Of memory; for who believes that older life, a wraith,
Maybe, but therefore more compelling, was the game
Made out by history where truth finds hard to grow?

That ignorance demands its opposite to appear
Is my assumption and defence, and I who walk
On this land, theirs and mine, build up this verse
In memory of a building and some fields with atmosphere
Where others walked, a family with its failures and a sparse
Success like others who have made the neighbours talk.

I do not, in spite of that, attempt to celebrate
An acceptable similarity. I point to difference,
From which we learn only what is there to learn,
That dignity which comes in every age to irritate
The general man to envy, though he may earn
Such insight as follows on subjective violence.

Different, they painted, made music, rode to hounds,
Were leisured, were farmers, colonels, baronets.
Men that we know today grow to be more or much the same,
But in an age of doubt of art, of houses without grounds.
The difference is not in titles but in a dignity that can shame,
A living pride that walks independent of an army's bayonets.

And so the histories make firm the history they deride
In telling of such houses and possessions of a class.
And so it is time we heard an end of what
We still call justice when our eager pride
In justice causes bloodshed even now, and rifle-shot
And rope still ply, and blood still trickles in Time's glass.

Where there is claim of truth and yet no peace
On either side of this larger, severed land,
Conscience must speak again. Yet as I walk,
My shadow rises on the new white wall: ideas cease
Their interaction; and here's an end to talk.
Above me a curtain is drawn by an age-old, steady hand.

But light from both window and moon has wakened a bird
Which sings a daylight song to this counterfeit.
The shadow pauses in the window: what is the song re-telling?
That heart's props change us, as house its owner, as will the word
Its farthest neighbour? Let me pray, as this dreaming dwelling
Must awake to new young, that these few properties stay complete.

O'REILLY'S REPLY

LET's say I live here, at any rate,
In the carefully careless country of England,
Where the humans are countless as a drift of sand,
Where John Betjeman shares in the trying confusions
Of young men who can sell their angry allusions
To the illusion of living in the Wellfed State.

Let's say I lose here, in a sense,
The sense of a freedom to live and die.
Where I come from, they either fight or multiply.
Here, in a country which once had charm,
The peasant walks in tweeds and does no one harm
And talks without a trace of innocence.

Let's say I love here, in a way,
Where the poet perfecting his poems before dark
May pick his writing-paper from the litter in the park.
Perhaps the place is like a hundred other places
Where a traffic-light only can stop the flow of faces.
Perhaps it's unlikely, but I'd like to stay.

THE LION AND O'REILLY

'WHO'LL rage against all government
That leaves the heart unheeded?'
'Who'll not?' cried out O'Reilly,
As he beat on the bar, unheeded.

'I've heard that said these fifty years
And still we're governmented',
Murmured a man with dulling eyes,
But no one else assented.

'The heart's a thing won't let us down;
The head is too confusing.
Who thinks about his heart too much
Will find himself refusing.'

'But the mind is strong when the heart is
And red blood fills the veins.
So up and rinse your minds, boys,
With life-blood till it pains.'

'A fight was fought some years ago
For freedom from the Lion.
Why should we now be roared at by
Some tyrant named O'Ryan?'

'We'll make a way for freedom
By thinking of bigger things
Than officials with their inkpot skulls
And forms with long green strings.'

'Who'll move this motion with me?
Who'll first and second it?'
'Who'll not?' cried out O'Reilly
Splitting the board with a final hit.

IN MEMORIAM

I. *Elizabeth At Twenty*

IT was only two fields away from the house
That the young Elizabeth
Offered so brazenly to the descending sun
Her two bronzed breasts,
And only towards nightfall
That she withdrew to a hedge
To dress. To dress again
At a quarter to eight
For what she would later
Describe in her diary as:
'This wholly immodest exhibition of bust,
Among all the other busts,
Upright and pointing about the dining-room table.'

II. *Elizabeth In Italy*

'SUDDENLY she slapped me, hard across the face.
I implored, but she declined to have any further
Social or sexual (so she put it) intercourse with me.
Neither would she give me either a personal picture
Or a lock of her most beautiful hair.
Indeed, she demanded, her exquisite voice
Quite hard, the return of her handkerchief
And any other things (I murmured, "mementoes",
But she repeated "things") I might have stolen
From her in my privileged position as her servant.
God only knew what had made her ask me
Fetch her the bathrobe that terrible night.
("That beautiful night", I recollected aloud.)
Did I believe our positions were reversed?

124

(I whitened at the accusation.) Well, then,
She wished to make clear now and for so long
As the relationship ("Madam!", cried I) lasted,
That it could only do so if I went to bed first,
Where she would come at her pleasure.
I could make no clearer sign of my heartfelt
Gratitude and infinite relief at these words
Than by the impassioned and repeated kissing,
There and then, of her magnificent left breast
Which had come out of hiding towards the end
Of her peroration. Whereupon she slapped me again.'

III. *Interruption At The Dance*

HAVING dreamed of a girl with bright red hair
And lightly freckled skin,
He is here to be seen
Picking his victim from the crowded dance-floor.

Now he contacts her,
Dances with her,
Guides her to an exit,
Is about to order a taxi
When the black-haired Elizabeth, crying,
'Margaret, who's that you've got there?',
Arrives to distract, attract
And tuck him into her waiting *Minotaur*.

Inside, he subsides into a passing lethargy,
Only later assenting to the white, pocked skin,
Recollecting, reflecting that this, after all,
Had always been the way of his waking-life.

IV. *In Memoriam*

Here the Antheme doth commence,
Love and Constancie is dead,
Phoenix and the Turtle fled,
In a mutuall flame from hence.

This lady, who had two motor-cars,
Three thousand articles of clothing
And no time for her husband,
Has left all behind her
For the next life.
Where, without doubt, she will regain
At least and at long last
Her long-lost independence.

Her husband, the black-haired Antony,
Is dutifully suspected by some friends
Of having bought another house
In the country, discreetly screened,
As so often before, by tall trees;
Because for three whole,
Wholly uneventful days,
He has not laid hands on a local woman.

THE FLIGHT OF THE WILD GEESE

FURTHER and farther flap the great grey geese,
Through the trailing sky, beyond long limp clouds
That thin away into the distant historical evening
In silent indication of where the sun has sunk;
Further and farther till the eyes strain and fail,
And the island of Ireland recedes and dims and dies
To a dream of dreams for more than two hundred years.

THE WAVE

ROCKS unfurl.
Unfolding, the view
Fades as it is caught.
Calling, the birds
Turn and beget
Endlessness so easily
I am afraid, stilled
Here with shells
Held in my hands.
The thundering sea
Softens as it reaches
The receiving sand,
Leaves, as it returns,
A thin band
Of fading foam
Over which two
Lovers are walking.
Calling above the roar,
Their voices reach me
Only as whispers,
Disturbing only
The turning birds
Into silence.
Silent and troubled,
These thoughts fly back
And back again
Along the sea's edge,
Awaiting impatiently,
Yet hesitantly,
The wave's returning.

SUMMA THEOLOGICA

THE time appointed,
His thought upright,
The husband claims
His awful right.

While his passive wife,
As she bares her skin,
Thinks: thus are we all
Borne in with sin.

And this is what
Saint Thomas teaches.
How else could our
Salvation reach us?

A LIFE

A DESOLATE chaos filled his days.
He could not pray, could not praise.
Life and a lover, he thought again,
Yet knew he could not bear that pain.

Rising to try each lying day
He saw there was nothing left to say.
Even in dreams the evening light
Would stop before becoming night.

One day he walked into the sea,
Nor fought nor felt it wrong to be
Drowning down his life's memories;
Knowing no courage was required in these.

ON AN ITALIAN HILLSIDE

On a hillside in Italy
The air shook like a single grass
In a secret morning wind
That moves no other about it
And moves it only,
Awaiting the waiting thoughts and themes of the day.

From a hillside in Italy
The sea was a child's blue slate
With toy craft signing their furrows
In chalk-marks, moved
By no child's hand, appearing,
Scratching in silence the tilted slate of the sea.

Above a hillside in Italy
The sun sank like a paper rose
Through water, dyeing it red,
Or like a drop of scarlet
Watercolour falling and softening
Into the yellow on already wet watercolour paper.

Below a hillside in Italy
The darkness filled the bay
Like flood-water, pushing
Down all opposition, submerging
The ships, the olive trees, the town,
The little gripping houses, the slipping rocks.

On a hillside in Italy
The lights came out like stars, steadied
In the net of haze over the sea.
And night climbed the hill to the top
To sit watching the twinkling fishboats
On the secret, slate-dark, flowering, flooded sea.

THE TRAVELLERS

THEN so dreadfully open and hoping.
Eyes wide. Then I betrayed you, afraid
Of taking and giving all. The fall of all
The future into my arms. And your charm
Retired behind tired sunlight
To a point of fear of an old joint
Union-betrayal. An old tale of failure
Of lovers trying to love. Trying.

You turned your face away to the sea,
And I drowned down into that sea.
Until the cold wind spoke and woke me.
You were still there, not crying, sighing,
Saying anything not kind. But your blind
Eyes watched and despatched me more firmly
Than a farewell could. We stood up
And went together down the hill to home.

FOR THE MOMENT

THE wretched lost rejected lover
Who cries tears—and at his age;

The writer who stares all night,
White-faced, at the white page;

The paradoxical philosopher who discovers
That his reasons are not reasonable;

The hurt wife who picks at her hurt
Until it becomes a kind of heart-trouble:

All know that life cannot be good
Unless they should imagine death
Arriving for them at that moment.

Love, hate, life, reason, the instant
Of intake of another new breath,
Can then, in that moment, be understood.

SELECTED LIST OF PUBLICATIONS

AUSTIN CLARKE
Collected Poems, 1935
Later Poems, 1961

RICHARD KELL
The Fantasy Press Poets No. 35, 1956
Control Tower, 1962

THOMAS KINSELLA
Poems, 1956
Another September, 1958
Moralities, 1960
Downstream, 1962

JOHN MONTAGUE
Forms of Exile, 1958
Poisoned Lands, 1961

RICHARD MURPHY
The Archaeology of Love, 1955
The Woman of the House, 1959
The Last Galway Hooker, 1961
Sailing to an Island, 1963

RICHARD WEBER
The Time Being, 1957
O'Reilly, 1957
Song for St. Stephen's Day, 1958
Lady and Gentleman, 1962

PRINTED IN GREAT BRITAIN
AT THE UNIVERSITY PRESS, OXFORD
BY VIVIAN RIDLER
PRINTER TO THE UNIVERSITY